Surviving A Layoff
by Harry Dahlstrom

Surviving A Layoff

ISBN 978-0-940712-99-7

Printed in the United States of America

Published by
Dahlstrom & Company, Inc.
50 October Hill Road
Holliston, MA 01746
Tel: 1-800-222-0009
www.DahlstromCo.com

Cover photography
Getty Images
Copyright, Milos Luzanin

Design
ChrisHerronDesign.com

Special thanks to
Deb Holmes, Ann Keenan, Jamie Dahlstrom, Gail Dahlstrom,
Chris Herron, Susan Plawsky, Andy Peterson, Lindsay
Dahlstrom, and the office pooches Bruce and Scout

Free job-hunting tools and the latest national hiring trends at
www.HarryDahlstrom.com

Contents

It's not your fault

You didn't do anything wrong. Losing your job because you were laid off is not your fault. Don't confuse a layoff with a firing. They are two different things.

Q. "What's the difference between a firing and a layoff?"

Firings remove people. Layoffs remove positions.

People who are fired usually did something to deserve losing their job— like theft, chronic absenteeism, or refusing to do the work.

People who are laid off did nothing wrong. Their job ended, usually because there wasn't enough work, the job or shift was abolished, or the plant closed.

Q. "What if I handled the news badly?"

Everybody takes the news differently. Some clam up and say nothing. Some plead and beg. Some sob and cry. Some get angry and say things they later regret. Some are glad and can't wait to start something new.

The person who told you that you were being laid off is a professional. He or she knows that losing a job is traumatic and that people react emotionally, not rationally. They try not to take your reaction personally.

After a week or so, if you still feel guilty about how you reacted when the manager gave you the news, consider sending her a short note. Simply say that you were surprised by the news and that you became emotional. Say that you regret taking out your feelings on her.

A short, hand-written apology says more about your character than all the tears and cursing of that emotionally charged meeting.

You're not alone. During 2016, approximately 20 million people lost their jobs. That's about 1.7 million people each month.

—U.S. Bureau of Labor Statistics

Q. "How am I going to tell my family?"

Say it clearly. Try not to be dramatic or timid.

You might say, "I have sad news about my job. I've been laid off. The layoff is effective today and the decision is final."

Stress that you were laid off, not fired, and that the decision is final.

Layoffs are emotional and you'll want to talk about it. So, explain what happened—who laid you off, where they did it, what they said, how they said it, how you felt, and what you said to them.

Mention the names of the other people who were laid off with you, as well as those who were not, and how everyone felt.

Introduce some hope. Tell your family that lots of people find new jobs in just a few months and many also find better jobs.

Plus, if you were burnt out by the kind of work you've been doing, now is a great time to look into a new line of work.

Q. "How am I going to make ends meet?"

Try not to worry about your finances today. Put it off for a day or two. Later, we'll show you how to handle your bills until you get on your feet again.

Q. "I'm a wreck over this."

Each of us lives in a "comfort zone." A comfort zone is an emotional place. It's a place where your work, your coworkers, and the demands of your job are routine and comfortable.

Suddenly, your "comfort zone" has been smashed and you can't fix it. You're in a mild state of shock.

As you can see from the chart on the right, losing your job is stressful. It's right up there with learning that you have a serious illness.

Most of us will need a few weeks to heal and get back on our feet. Those who were deeply wounded by the layoff might need a few months to heal.

During this healing time, each of us will experience four different emotions. Turn the page—we need to talk about them.

COMPARING LIFE'S MAJOR STRESSES

If losing your spouse is the greatest stress, how do other stressful situations compare? Here's a partial list:

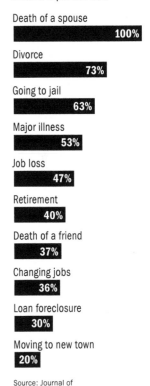

Death of a spouse — 100%
Divorce — 73%
Going to jail — 63%
Major illness — 53%
Job loss — 47%
Retirement — 40%
Death of a friend — 37%
Changing jobs — 36%
Loan foreclosure — 30%
Moving to new town — 20%

Source: Journal of Psychosomatic Research

Take time to heal

People react differently to losing their job. Some can shrug it off as if nothing happened. Some need time to grieve. A few are so wounded, they may need a little help.

Q. "I'll be okay. I just need some time."

Time is important in the grieving process.

Q. "Grieving process, what's that?"

Whenever we lose something that's important to us, we grieve. Grieving is an emotional process that helps us cope with our loss. It has four basic stages:

- **Shock.** A disbelief that this has happened to you.

- **Anger.** A feeling that you have been wronged.

- **Mourning.** A sadness and longing for what is gone.

- **Acceptance.** The eventual desire to get on with your life.

Q. "Shock. I'll admit it. I was shocked by the layoff. I didn't see it coming."

Most people can handle the shock. It usually wears off in a few days.

But, some have difficulty with it and do irrational things.

Some escape by going on huge spending sprees or taking expensive vacations when they should be conserving their finances. Others rush to return their new TV, car, or furniture and cancel the debt.

Try not to make any important decisions for a few days. Instead, give the shock a few days to wear off. Try to relax. Do the things you normally love to do. Spend some time with your family. Take a day trip. Read a novel. Clean the garage. Get away from "the job."

If you have thoughts of hurting yourself or hurting someone else, pick up a phone and dial 911. Help is only a phone call away.

Q. "Anger. Do I have a right to be angry?"

Yes, you do. Anger is a natural emotion. Once the shock of losing your job wears off, you're going to feel it.

In your anger, you may fantasize about punching the boss in the nose, filing a lawsuit, or writing a letter to the newspapers.

Fantasizing is one thing. Following through is another.

Keep in mind, that you are going to need another job. If you file a frivolous lawsuit, write libelous letters, or assault someone—it could haunt you for decades. Background checking is big business these days. Future employers will learn about your mischief and they will shun you.

Instead, find a good sounding board. A sounding board is someone who will listen to your complaints—over and over again.

Don't use your spouse, parents, or kids as a sounding board, though. They'll get sick of it.

The best sounding boards are people who have also lost their jobs. Find those fellow victims. Get together, scream, shout, cry, and vent that anger together.

Q. "Mourning. I'm going to miss my friends."

So give them a call or meet them for lunch. Stay in touch.

Don't forget those other people who were laid off with you—the grumpy lady who ran the copier, the funny guy who worked in payroll, and that kid with the tattoos who taught you all those computer tricks.

Get in touch with them too. Tell them you were thinking about them. Ask how they're doing. Feed them some encouragement. You'll feel good for reaching out and they'll think you're special because you cared.

Then, try this—send two hand-written notes, one to your old boss and the other to the CEO of the company. Thank them for your old job and all the great things you learned there. Add a short personal story about an opportunity you were given and what it meant to you.

When you need a reference for a new job, that note will speak volumes about your character.

Q. "Acceptance. How long will it take for me to get over all of this?"

Everybody's different. Some experts think most of us need several weeks to cycle through the grieving process.

But, if you still have difficulty coping with daily life two weeks after losing your job, you may be suffering from clinical depression.

Clinical depression is a serious but treatable illness. Some of the symptoms include: low energy, poor appetite, can't sleep, feeling worthless, feeling hopeless, can't concentrate, blaming yourself.

If you have several of these symptoms two weeks after losing your job, call your doctor.

Q. "Right now, my biggest worry is money."

Okay, let's talk about money. Flip the page.

ON THE HOME FRONT

This is a touchy subject. Like it or not, here it is.

Some men who lose their jobs become jealous of their working wives. They no longer see themselves as breadwinners. So, they belittle their spouses and minimize the importance of their jobs.

Then too, some wives become resentful of their unemployed husbands. They see themselves single-handedly supporting the family and it can seem overwhelming.

When you're itching for an argument, get out of the house and go for a brisk walk. A brisk walk can calm the frustration, physically as well as emotionally. You might also call a laid-off friend and tell them how you feel. They know what you're going through and they're usually willing to listen.

Women who lose their jobs cope better than men. They are less likely to resent their working husbands.

Jealousy almost always stems from a lowered self-esteem. That is, not thinking you're very important.

The best way to handle jealousy is to talk about it. Find out what's expected of you, what's expected of them, and create some "temporary roles."

Then, make an effort to show respect for the other person and how they might feel.

How to pay your bills when you have no paycheck

Money. Here's a subject that really scares unemployed people. Now, before you panic, take a deep breath and relax. We're going to walk through your money problems and show you a few things you might not know—things that could make your hard times a bit more bearable.

Q. "Where do I start?"

The first thing you need to do is to sign up for unemployment-insurance benefits from your state.

Q. "Oh, I'd be embarrassed to sign up for benefits."

Don't be. The government requires employers to buy unemployment insurance for their employees. This insurance provides a financial cushion for employees who lose their jobs.

It's insurance, not a handout. Your employer paid for this insurance. Don't be embarrassed about signing up.

Q. "How do I file a claim?"

Each state has different rules for eligibility. So, call your local benefits office and ask how to file a claim. You can find their telephone number by Googling "unemployment insurance" and your state's name. Or, look in the "Business Section" of your telephone book. They're listed under your state's name: "Massachusetts › Employment › Unemployment Insurance."

When you call, the benefits agent will ask a few questions to see whether you qualify to receive benefits. So, have the following information handy—your Social Security Number or alien registration number if you are not a citizen, your last day of employment, your employer's

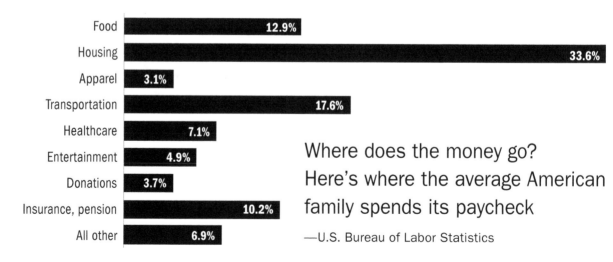

Food — 12.9%
Housing — 33.6%
Apparel — 3.1%
Transportation — 17.6%
Healthcare — 7.1%
Entertainment — 4.9%
Donations — 3.7%
Insurance, pension — 10.2%
All other — 6.9%

Where does the money go? Here's where the average American family spends its paycheck

—U.S. Bureau of Labor Statistics

name and address, and the reason you are no longer working.

Q. "How much money will I get?"

It depends on how much money you earned while working and how long you worked. Plus, each state pays different amounts and the amounts change year to year. The benefits agent will explain how much you are qualified to receive when you register.

Keep in mind, though, these benefits are only a financial cushion—they will not replace your full paycheck.

Q. "I don't even know how much money I'll need every month."

Use the worksheet on the right to tally up the numbers. It's as easy as 1...2...3...

Q. "What if I don't have enough income to make ends meet?"

Then, you'll have to dip into your savings.

So, remember that emergency fund with three-months pay that you stashed away for a rainy day? Well, it's raining. You're going to need that money to make ends meet.

Huh? You never got around to creating that emergency fund?

You have four options:

1. Reduce your spending and live within your new means.
2. Find extra money to reduce your cash gap.
3. Ask your creditors to reduce your bills until you find another job.
4. Get help from a non-profit credit counselor.

For details, turn the page—

REVIEW YOUR FINANCES

1. Add up your monthly income

Unemployment Benefit	$ _____
Spouse's Paycheck	_____
Other Income	_____
Total Income [1]	$ _____

2. List your monthly expenses

Figure what you spend monthly for each of the following items. On credit cards, list your current minimum monthly payment.

Rent or Mortgage	$ _____
Heat	_____
Light	_____
Phone	_____
Food	_____
Clothing	_____
Insurance	_____
Taxes	_____
Auto Loan	_____
Credit Card	_____
Credit Card	_____
Credit Card	_____
Other Loan	_____
Donations	_____
Medical, Healthcare	_____
Transportation	_____
Entertainment	_____
Other	_____
Total Expenses [2]	$ _____

3. Establish the gap

Subtract your Total Expenses[2] from your Total Income[1] to see whether you have a positive or a negative cash flow.

Total Income [1]	$ _____
Total Expenses [2]	— _____
The Cash Gap	$ _____

REDUCE YOUR SPENDING

Go frugal

Turn off the lights and the TV when you're not using them. Put a full load in the washer and clothes dryer. When it's cold, set the thermostat to 68° and put on a sweater. In the summer, use a fan when it's hot. If you find a great price on gasoline—fill up your car's gas tank.

Stop carrying your credit cards

Pay with cash. Can't part with your credit cards, try this: Fill a one-gallon plastic container with water. Put all your credit cards in the container of water. Put the container in the freezer. Freeze your spending.

Plan a weekly meal menu

Prepare a list of the foods you'll need for that menu. Clip discount coupons from the newspapers and store circulars. Did you know we throw away over $100 a month in discount coupons? Shop aggressively for the best price and bring only enough cash to pay for the things on your list. Buy the store brands. Before you get to the checkout counter, put back 10 percent of the things in your basket— especially snacks, beverages, and prepared foods.

Stay away from restaurants

We spend about 13 percent of our total income on food. Almost half that amount is spent in restaurants, snack bars, vending machines, and fast food joints. Eat at home or brown-bag a lunch.

Stay away from the malls

Americans visit some kind of a mall at least twice a week. A lot of us have the notion that shopping is some form of entertainment—it's not. If you have to go to a mall, bring a list of the things you truly need and bring only enough cash to buy what's on your list.

Trim your entertainment

Americans spend a lot of money on entertainment each month—movie rentals, cable TV, sports, hobbies, toys, and lottery tickets—just to name a few. Cut back until you find a new job.

HOW TO CUT THE FAT OUT OF YOUR SPENDING

Here's a more detailed list of personal expenses. Figure what you spend monthly on each item. Then, cut the fat and create a spending plan you can live with while you're out of work.

	Old Habits — Enter your average monthly spending for each item ▼	New Cuts — How much could you cut from each item every month ▼	New Spending — Subtract New Cuts from Old Habits to find your new spending limit ▼
Groceries	$_____	$_____	$_____
Dining Out	_____	_____	_____
Rent/Mortgage	_____	_____	_____
Household	_____	_____	_____
Heat	_____	_____	_____
Electricity	_____	_____	_____
Telephone	_____	_____	_____
Clothing	_____	_____	_____
Medical	_____	_____	_____
Barber, Beauty	_____	_____	_____
Entertainment	_____	_____	_____
Gifts	_____	_____	_____
Auto Loans	_____	_____	_____
Auto Gas, Tolls	_____	_____	_____
Public Transit	_____	_____	_____
Credit Card	_____	_____	_____
Credit Card	_____	_____	_____
Credit Card	_____	_____	_____
Other Loans	_____	_____	_____
Insurance	_____	_____	_____
Taxes	_____	_____	_____
Education	_____	_____	_____
Savings	_____	_____	_____
Other	_____	_____	_____
TOTALS	$_____	$_____	$_____

FIND EXTRA MONEY TO REDUCE THE CASH GAP

Collect old debts

Stop and think—does anyone owe you money? If someone owes you money, now is the time to ask for it. If they don't have the cash to repay you, put them on a time payment plan. Get them to make weekly or monthly payments to you until the debt is repaid.

Turn unwanted things into gold

Take a walk through your home and take an inventory of the things you no longer need or use—baby furniture, old kitchen set, golf clubs, air conditioner, power tools, stereo equipment, cameras, musical instruments. Look through your closets, basement, attic, garage, or storage space too. Run an ad on eBay or in the classified section of your local newspaper and unload those unwanted things for cash.

Turn stuff into gold

If you have boxes of stuff that aren't worth the cost of advertising, have a yard sale or a sidewalk sale. People are always willing to spend a few bucks on books, clothes, hand tools, toys, dishes, lamps, fans, appliances, and anything else of small value.
To pull in the paying customers, wait for a nice weekend, pile the stuff outside where people passing by can see it, and hang a "yard sale" sign out front and at the street corners.

Unload the family jewels

Do you have valuables that you'd like to sell? If you have jewelry, a coin collection, silver service, a gold watch, antique furniture or rugs—have them appraised. After you get the written appraisal, ask the appraiser to recommend the best way to sell the item.
If the items have strong sentimental value, offer them to your relatives first.

Change your lifestyle

Are you living beyond your means? Are your home, your car, or your dining habits leaving you broke? A smaller home, a smaller car, and more home-cooked meals could leave you healthier, wealthier, and wiser.

HOW TO CASH IN ON YOURSELF

1. Do you have a talent or skill?

Can you give music lessons, write resumes, take wedding photos, draw or illustrate, decorate cakes, tutor students, create web sites, network computers, sew or do alterations?

What talents do you have that people or local businesses might need?

_____

_____

2. Do you have any free time?

You don't need a special talent to make extra money on your own. Lots of people are looking for someone to do odd or routine jobs—babysit, run errands, check on an elderly relative, prepare a meal, clean things, move things, fix things, pull weeds, detail the car, or walk the dog.
What services could you offer?

_____

_____

3. Now, bring in the paying customers:

· Use social media to get the word out to your friends

· List your service in local online bulletin boards, like Craigslist.org.

· Distribute flyers to homes and businesses in your area.

· Hang flyers on the bulletin boards at supermarkets, places of worship, and community centers.

· Leave a flyer beneath the windshield wiper of cars parked on the street.

· Ask friends to refer you to their friends and employers.

CALL YOUR CREDITORS AND ASK TO HAVE YOUR BILLS REDUCED

Job loss is a real crisis

Your creditors know how devastating a job loss, illness, divorce, or a natural disaster can be. Don't feel embarrassed or ashamed about losing your job. The layoff was beyond your control. What does matter is how you handle your hardship. If you inform your creditors early on, and ask for help, they'll work with you. But, if you say nothing and force them to come looking for you, then they'll be less sympathetic when they learn about your hardship.

Call your creditors before they call you

Call all of your creditors: credit cards, auto loan, landlord, mortgage company, heat, light, phone, taxes—everybody. On your monthly bill, look for a statement like, "Billing Inquiries" or "Billing Errors." There should also be a toll free telephone number listed. Call that number and ask to speak with the credit manager.

Tell how much you can afford to pay

Don't let the credit managers set the amount that you must pay each month. Instead, tell them how much you can afford to pay. Use the worksheet on page 10 and figure what you can pay.

Everybody gets nervous

If you get nervous when talking to a credit manager—STOP. Take a deep breath—tell the manager that you are very nervous and that you've never asked for anything like this before. That will often bring a smile to the manager's face and she'll become more sympathetic.

Not a negotiator?

If you don't feel comfortable calling each of your creditors and negotiating a reduced monthly payment, you might ask a friend or a relative to call for you. But, if you don't want them to know all the details of your finances, ask a credit counselor for help. See page 13 for more information about credit counselors.

Important note

You need housing, heat, light, and food to survive. You need a telephone and a car to find a job. If money gets terribly tight and you cannot pay all your bills—pay those bills. Call everybody else and explain that they'll have to wait.

HOW TO TALK TO YOUR CREDITORS

Take the offensive: Call your creditors before they call you. Work out a reduced payment program. Before you call, be sure to have your current statement, account number, plus a pen and paper handy. Be friendly, courteous, but businesslike. Here's a script you can use:

1. Introduce yourself
"Good morning, Ms. Cashhold. My name is Bill Debt. Thank you for taking my call."

2. Get down to business
"Ms. Cashhold, six weeks ago I lost my job. I'm behind on my payments to you."

3. Ask for help
"I need some help. Could we arrange a special payment program until I get on my feet again?"

4. Prepare to negotiate
"I'm sorry, but I can't afford to pay that amount." "I have several other creditors that I'm also calling this morning. I can afford to pay you $XX a month. That's half my usual payment. At that rate, I can afford to make ends meet and you'll receive a steady monthly payment. In a few months, I should have another job and I'll resume making my full payments."

5. Get an agreement
"Thank you Ms. Cashhold. Yes, I understand. My credit privileges are suspended until I return to work. Until then, I'll pay $XX a month. You will call periodically to check on my employment status."

6. Thank the creditor
"Thank you for working with me, Ms. Cashhold. Please send me a written confirmation of our agreement."

GET HELP FROM A NON-PROFIT CREDIT COUNSELOR

You don't have to be in debt to get help from a credit counselor

But, if you are in debt, the sooner you call a credit counselor the better off you'll be. Sadly, too many people wait too long and the only option left is bankruptcy. So, if you lost your job, if you survived a natural disaster, if you went crazy and bought something you cannot afford—call a credit counselor. You'll be amazed at what they can do to help you.

Credit counselors are good listeners

A good credit counselor will listen to your story. She'll encourage you to talk and get things off your chest. She'll ask lots of questions. She'll tell you about other situations where people faced the same problems you face. She'll tell you what they did—what worked and what didn't work. She'll help you figure out a plan. She'll help you put that plan into action. She'll become your coach, your cheerleader, your friend.

Depending on your situation, credit counselors can—

- Create a plan that lets you live within your means
- Rebuild your reputation with your creditors
- Stop the collection calls and legal notices
- Reduce your monthly payments
- Reduce your interest rate
- Waive late fees
- Re-age your account so that it's not in default
- Consolidate all your bills into one payment
- Offer motivation, education, & encouragement
- Prevent bankruptcy

Counseling is surprisingly affordable

Counseling from a non-profit agency is usually free to the needy. The not-so-needy might be charged $75 for a one-hour counseling session.

Creditors prefer to work with a counselor

Over the years, credit counselors have built up solid relationships with local creditors. The counselors have a history, a track record, and a reputation that creditors trust. If a counselor calls a creditor on your behalf, it says that you are serious about taking control of your bill—and that's good enough for most creditors.

HOW TO CHOOSE A CREDIT COUNSELOR

All credit counselors are not the same. Some businesses masquerade as credit counselors but they're really selling debt consolidation loans, bankruptcy services, or debt negotiation programs.

Where to find a credit counselor

- The U.S. Bankruptcy Court maintains a list of their approved credit counseling agencies at— www.usdoj.gov/ust
- The National Foundation for Consumer Credit maintains links to their member agencies at— www.nfcc.org
- The Association of Independent Consumer Credit Counseling Agencies maintains links to their member agencies at —www.aiccca.org
- The Better Business Bureau can tell you if an agency has a history of consumer complaints— www.BBBonLine.org.

Call three agencies. Compare services and fees

Here are some questions to ask—with straight answers:

- Is your agency a non-profit organization? (Yes.)
- Is your agency licensed? (Yes.)
- Are your counselors certified or enrolled in a certification program? (Yes.)
- Will I receive a thorough financial interview, a written evaluation, a best-case solution, and education to help prevent future financial problems? (Yes.)
- How long will the session take? (About an hour.)
- What is the cost of the session? (About $75.)
- Are there any monthly fees for joining a DMP— Debt Management Program? (About $50 a month.)
- What if I can't pay your fees? (No one has ever been turned away due to an inability to pay.)
- Do you also offer affordable workshops, classes, or free educational material? (Yes.)
- Are your employees paid more if I sign up for certain services, such as a DMP? (No.)
- Would I get a written contract with free information about services, payment terms, total cost, and the time needed to achieve results? (Yes.)

This could be a good time to consider a new line of work

After losing their jobs, a lot of people think about switching to a new line of work. Whether you're happy with your current line of work or not, it's nice to know you have other options.

Q. "What kind of work should I switch to?"

First, you don't have to switch careers at all. If you're happy with the work you do, or if it's impractical for you to change careers, stay put. But, if you've ever wondered whether you are more suited to a different kind of work, now is the time to check.

Q. "Where do I start?"

· *Start with your wish list.* What kind of job excites you? What kind of job would you like to do if you could start your life all over again?

· *Think about your hobbies and interests.* Could you turn something you love into a new career?

· *Think of the things you can do.* Do you have a special talent, skill, or ability that you could turn into a career?

· *Think about the special knowledge you have.* Could you apply anything you know to a new career?

· *Think of the people you know.* Does someone have the kind of job that you'd like to have?

Q. "I'm not sure about any of those."

Would you like a more scientific approach to selecting a career? Log onto a computer and Google, "*career tests.*"

These career tests ask about 30 multiple-choice questions. They analyze your answers and come up with a personality profile. Then, they match your profile to several career fields that go well with your personality type.

Most of the tests are free, so give them a try. The results can be very interesting. One caution, however—no test is totally accurate. Take several tests and use the results only as a guide.

Q. "If I find a career that interests me, how can I learn more about it?"

First, turn to pages 16 and 17 in this book and

The Standard Occupational Classification System includes over 840 separate U.S. occupations.

—U.S. Department of Labor

get the scoop on the typical wages, demand, and training for that occupation.

Then, visit www.dol.gov. That's the U.S. Department of Labor's web site. Click on "Occupational Outlook Handbook." There, you'll find detailed job descriptions on hundreds of different occupations.

Once you've zeroed in on a career that excites you, go out and talk to people who work in that occupation. The idea is to learn what they like and dislike about their work.

To find someone who works in that job, talk to your friends, relatives, teachers, preachers, politicians, beautician, barber, realtor, police officers, and local business owners.

Ask if they know someone who works in the job you want. Then, ask if they would call that person and set up a telephone meeting for you so you can talk to them. Or, even better, meet them for a cup of coffee.

Q. "Is this for real—do people really get together and talk about their jobs?"

You bet they do. It's called "informational interviewing" and it's one of the best ways to learn about the real job.

Q. "What kind of questions should I ask this person?"

When you meet, be friendly and inquisitive. Here are some questions you might ask:

- How did you get into this line of work?
- What are your duties and responsibilities?
- What skills are needed to do this job?
- Tell me about your typical day at work.
- What do you like most about what you do? Why?
- What do you dislike most about what you do? How do you cope?

- What do employers really look for when hiring?
- Who are the major local employers?
- Does the future look healthy for employment in this field?
- Any advice for someone looking for a first-time job in this field?

After the meeting, be sure to send a short thank-you note to the person you met as well as the person who introduced you. These people might become important contacts when you begin searching for a job.

Q. "Is there some way I could talk to a career counselor?"

Absolutely. Did you know that there are over 2,000 American Job Centers across the USA? They've helped millions of people find work—and their services are free and open to the public.

Call or visit your local Job Center and make an appointment to speak with an employment counselor. To find a local office, Google *American Job Centers* or *One-Stop Career Centers*.

Your counselor will begin by asking questions about your work interests. She might also ask you to take a career test to uncover possibilities you aren't aware of. The counselor could then explain the local opportunities for your career choices—who the major employers are, which skills they want, and how to develop a job-hunting plan. If you need job training or retraining, she can recommend several approved providers.

Now, employment counselors have worked with lots of people and they have lots of contacts. So, ask your counselor if she could arrange for you to talk with someone who works in the job you want. You could learn a lot in a 15-20 minute telephone chat.

If you like what you hear, ask your counselor if she could arrange an authorized tour inside a company so you could experience the job in action.

WHAT ARE THE PROS AND CONS OF YOUR NEW CAREER?

Will you enjoy the work for the mere pleasure of doing it?
YES ☐   NO ☐

Will the work be interesting enough that problems become challenges instead of frustrations?
YES ☐   NO ☐

Is the product or service you'll offer needed, worthwhile, and reputable?
YES ☐   NO ☐

Are the people you'll work with and the customers you'll serve, the kind of people you'll be proud to be associated with?
YES ☐   NO ☐

Will you feel respected for the work you do?
YES ☐   NO ☐

Will you make a comfortable wage and be able to provide your family with the things they want and need?
YES ☐   NO ☐

Are there opportunities for personal and professional growth in this field?
YES ☐   NO ☐

Is this a growing occupation with a good outlook for employment? (See pages 16 and 17)
YES ☐   NO ☐

Wages & Demand for America's Top 175 Occupations, 2014-2024

Jobs are created in two ways, by replacement and growth. *Replacement:* These are job openings to replace people who have left or changed jobs. Replacement accounts for about 6 out of every 10 hires. *Growth:* These are job openings created when a new business starts up or an existing business expands. Growth accounts for about 4 out of every 10 hires.

Education & Training Codes

- SH = Some High School
- HS = High School Diploma or Equivalent
- PS = Postsecondary Non-Degree Award
- SC = Some College, No Degree
- AD = Associate's Degree
- BD = Bachelor's Degree
- MA = Master's Degree
- DP = Doctoral or Professional Degree

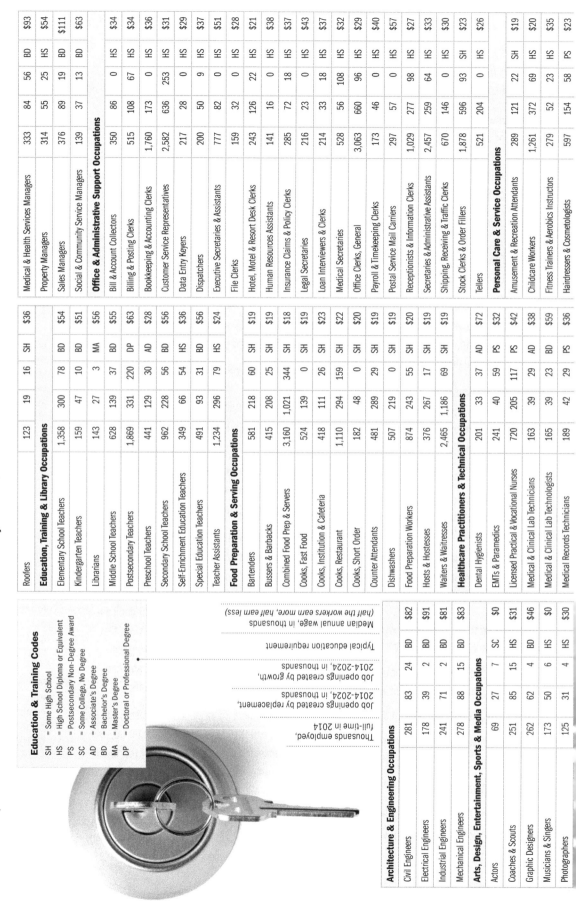

Column key:

- **Employed** — Thousands employed, full-time in 2014
- **Replacement** — Job openings created by replacement, 2014-2024, in thousands
- **Growth** — Job openings created by growth, 2014-2024, in thousands
- **Education** — Typical education requirement
- **Wage** — Median annual wage, in thousands (half the workers earn more, half earn less)

Occupation	Employed	Replacement	Growth	Education	Wage
Roofers	123	19	16	SH	$36
Education, Training & Library Occupations					
Elementary School Teachers	1,358	300	78	BD	$54
Kindergarten Teachers	159	47	10	BD	$51
Librarians	143	27	3	MA	$56
Middle School Teachers	628	139	37	BD	$55
Postsecondary Teachers	1,869	331	220	DP	$63
Preschool Teachers	441	129	30	AD	$28
Secondary School Teachers	962	228	56	BD	$56
Self-Enrichment Education Teachers	349	66	54	HS	$36
Special Education Teachers	491	93	31	BD	$56
Teacher Assistants	1,234	296	79	HS	$24
Food Preparation & Serving Occupations					
Bartenders	581	218	60	SH	$19
Bussers & Barbacks	415	208	25	SH	$19
Combined Food Prep & Servers	3,160	1,021	344	SH	$18
Cooks, Fast Food	524	139	0	SH	$19
Cooks, Institution & Cafeteria	418	111	26	SH	$23
Cooks, Restaurant	1,110	294	159	SH	$22
Cooks, Short Order	182	48	0	SH	$20
Counter Attendants	481	289	29	SH	$19
Dishwashers	507	219	0	SH	$19
Food Preparation Workers	874	243	55	SH	$20
Hosts & Hostesses	376	267	17	SH	$19
Waiters & Waitresses	2,465	1,186	69	SH	$19
Healthcare Practitioners & Technical Occupations					
Dental Hygienists	201	33	37	AD	$72
EMTs & Paramedics	241	40	59	PS	$32
Licensed Practical & Vocational Nurses	720	205	117	PS	$42
Medical & Clinical Lab Technicians	163	39	29	AD	$38
Medical & Clinical Lab Technologists	165	39	23	BD	$59
Medical Records Technicians	189	42	29	PS	$36

Occupation	Employed	Replacement	Growth	Education	Wage
Medical & Health Services Managers	333	84	56	BD	$93
Property Managers	314	55	25	HS	$54
Sales Managers	376	89	19	BD	$111
Social & Community Service Managers	139	37	13	BD	$63
Office & Administrative Support Occupations					
Bill & Account Collectors	350	86	0	HS	$34
Billing & Posting Clerks	515	108	67	HS	$34
Bookkeeping & Accounting Clerks	1,760	173	0	HS	$36
Customer Service Representatives	2,582	636	253	HS	$31
Data Entry Keyers	217	28	0	HS	$29
Dispatchers	200	50	9	HS	$37
Executive Secretaries & Assistants	777	82	0	HS	$51
File Clerks	159	32	0	HS	$28
Hotel, Motel & Resort Desk Clerks	243	126	22	HS	$21
Human Resources Assistants	141	16	0	HS	$38
Insurance Claims & Policy Clerks	285	72	18	HS	$37
Legal Secretaries	216	23	0	HS	$43
Loan Interviewers & Clerks	214	33	18	HS	$37
Medical Secretaries	528	56	108	HS	$32
Office Clerks, General	3,063	660	96	HS	$29
Payroll & Timekeeping Clerks	173	46	0	HS	$40
Postal Service Mail Carriers	297	57	0	HS	$57
Receptionists & Information Clerks	1,029	277	98	HS	$27
Secretaries & Administrative Assistants	2,457	259	64	HS	$33
Shipping, Receiving & Traffic Clerks	670	146	0	HS	$30
Stock Clerks & Order Fillers	1,878	596	93	SH	$23
Tellers	521	204	0	HS	$26
Personal Care & Service Occupations					
Amusement & Recreation Attendants	289	121	22	SH	$19
Childcare Workers	1,261	372	69	HS	$20
Fitness Trainers & Aerobics Instructors	279	52	23	HS	$35
Hairdressers & Cosmetologists	597	154	58	PS	$23

Occupation	Employed	Replacement	Growth	Education	Wage
Architecture & Engineering Occupations					
Civil Engineers	281	83	24	BD	$82
Electrical Engineers	178	39	2	BD	$91
Industrial Engineers	241	71	2	BD	$81
Mechanical Engineers	278	88	15	BD	$83
Arts, Design, Entertainment, Sports & Media Occupations					
Actors	69	27	7	SC	$0
Coaches & Scouts	251	85	15	HS	$31
Graphic Designers	262	62	4	BD	$46
Musicians & Singers	173	50	6	HS	$0
Photographers	125	31	4	HS	$30

Building & Grounds Cleaning & Maintenance Occupations

Occupation				Ed.	Wage
Janitors & Cleaners	2,361	469	136	SH	$23
Landscapers & Groundskeepers	1,168	211	72	SH	$24
Maids & Housekeeping Cleaners	1,458	348	112	SH	$20

Business & Financial Operations Occupations

Occupation				Ed.	Wage
Accountants & Auditors	1,333	356	142	BD	$66
Claims Adjusters, Examiners & Investigators	300	74	10	HS	$62
Compliance Officers	260	37	9	BD	$65
Financial Analysts	278	57	32	BD	$79
Loan Officers	303	50	25	HS	$63
Management Analysts	758	105	103	BD	$81
Market Research Analysts	496	59	92	BD	$61
Personal Financial Advisors	249	63	74	BD	$81
Purchasing Agents	301	83	0	HS	$61

Community & Social Service Occupations

Occupation				Ed.	Wage
Child, Family & School Social Workers	305	74	19	BD	$42
Clergy	244	53	14	BD	$44
Guidance & Vocational Counselors	273	57	23	MA	$53
Healthcare Social Workers	160	39	31	MA	$52
Mental Health Counselors	135	28	26	MA	$41
Rehabilitation Counselors	120	25	11	MA	$34
Social & Human Service Assistants	387	76	44	HS	$30

Computer & Mathematical Occupations

Occupation				Ed.	Wage
Computer Programmers	329	81	0	BD	$78
Computer Support Specialists	767	99	89	SC	$50
Computer Systems Analysts	568	73	119	BD	$83
Network & Computer Systems Admins	383	49	30	BD	$76
Software Developers, Applications	718	103	135	BD	$96
Software Developers, System Software	396	57	51	BD	$103
Web Developers	149	19	39	AD	$63

Construction & Extraction Occupations

Occupation				Ed.	Wage
Carpenters	945	109	60	HS	$41
Cement Masons & Concrete Finishers	155	19	20	SH	$37
Construction Laborers	1,159	231	147	SH	$31
Electricians	629	96	86	HS	$51
Operating Engineers	363	61	37	HS	$44
Painters, Construction & Maintenance	361	57	27	SH	$36
Plumbers, Pipefitters & Steamfitters	425	56	49	HS	$51

Healthcare Practitioners

Occupation				Ed.	Wage
Physical Therapists	211	57	72	DP	$82
Physicians & Surgeons	708	191	99	DP	$187
Radiologic Technologists	197	37	17	AD	$56
Registered Nurses	2,751	649	439	AD	$67
Veterinarians	78	12	7	DP	$88

Healthcare Support Occupations

Occupation				Ed.	Wage
Dental Assistants	319	79	59	PS	$35
Home Health Aides	914	206	348	SH	$21
Massage Therapists	169	13	37	PS	$37
Medical Assistants	591	123	139	HS	$30
Nursing Assistants	2,536	573	620	PS	$24

Installation, Maintenance & Repair Occupations

Occupation				Ed.	Wage
Automotive Body & Related Repairers	150	34	14	HS	$40
Automotive Technicians & Mechanics	740	198	39	HS	$37
Bus & Truck Mechanics	264	45	32	HS	$44
HVAC&R Mechanics & Installers	292	45	40	PS	$45
Industrial Machinery Mechanics	332	86	60	HS	$49
Maintenance & Repair Workers	1,375	360	84	HS	$36
Telecom Equipment Installers & Repairers	219	20	0	PS	$55
Telecom Line Installers & Repairers	118	22	1	HS	$54

Legal Occupations

Occupation				Ed.	Wage
Judges & Magistrates	30	4	0	DP	$115
Lawyers	779	114	44	DP	$115
Paralegals & Legal Assistants	280	61	21	AD	$48

Management Occupations

Occupation				Ed.	Wage
Administrative Services Managers	287	54	24	HS	$84
Architectural & Engineering Managers	182	56	4	BD	$131
Chief Executives	343	58	0	BD	$173
Computer & Info. Systems Managers	349	41	54	BD	$128
Construction Managers	373	52	18	AD	$86
Education Administrators, K-12	240	70	14	MA	$90
Education Administrators, Postsecondary	175	51	15	MA	$88
Farm, Ranch & Agricultural Managers	930	158	0	HS	$68
Financial Managers	556	132	38	BD	$115
Food Service Managers	305	61	16	HS	$49
General & Operations Managers	2,124	538	151	AD	$97
Industrial Production Managers	173	49	0	BD	$92
Marketing Managers	194	46	18	BD	$127

Production Occupations

Occupation				Ed.	Wage
Cut, Punch & Press Machine Operators	192	24	0	HS	$31
Electrical Equipment Assemblers	207	26	0	HS	$30
Helpers, Production Workers	419	137	0	SH	$24
Inspectors, Testers, Sorters & Weighers	497	125	0	HS	$35
Laundry & Dry-Cleaning Workers	208	30	4	SH	$20
Machinists	400	116	39	HS	$40
Meat, Poultry & Fish Cutters & Trimmers	152	30	0	SH	$23
Packaging & Filling Machine Operators	378	135	4	HS	$26
Printing Press Operators	173	26	0	HS	$35
Team Assemblers	1,144	246	0	HS	$28
Welders, Cutters, Solderers & Brazers	398	114	14	HS	$37

Protective Services Occupations

Occupation				Ed.	Wage
Correctional Officers & Jailers	453	120	22	HS	$39
Firefighters	307	84	20	PS	$45
Police & Sheriff's Patrol Officers	654	205	39	HS	$55
Security Guards	1,074	165	130	HS	$24

Sales & Related Occupations

Occupation				Ed.	Wage
Cashiers	3,424	1,457	67	SH	$19
Counter & Rental Clerks	442	109	16	SH	$24
Insurance Sales Agents	466	122	43	HS	$48
Parts Salespersons	235	52	17	SH	$29
Real Estate Sales Agents	337	24	10	HS	$41
Retail Salespersons	4,625	1,603	314	SH	$21
Sales Reps, Wholesale & Manufacturing	1,453	299	93	HS	$55
Securities & Financial Sales Agents	342	59	33	BD	$72
Telemarketers	238	44	0	SH	$23

Transportation & Material Moving Occupations

Occupation				Ed.	Wage
Bus Drivers, School or Special Client	497	65	28	HS	$29
Bus Drivers, Transit & Intercity	168	22	10	HS	$37
Driver/Sales Workers	445	76	21	HS	$22
Heavy & Tractor-Trailer Truck Drivers	1,798	306	99	HS	$40
Industrial Truck & Tractor Operators	531	132	13	SH	$31
Laborers & Material Movers, Hand	2,441	727	125	SH	$24
Light Truck or Delivery Drivers	885	151	27	HS	$30
Packers & Packagers, Hand	695	185	12	SH	$20
Refuse & Recyclable Material Collectors	132	33	9	SH	$34
Taxi Drivers & Chauffeurs	234	44	31	SH	$23

Show the employer that you have the "right stuff"

Every occupation has certain requirements. Carpenters must know how to read building plans. Sales people must know how to close a sale. Customer-service people must know how to work with difficult people. Managers must know how to motivate people to get the job done. What's the right stuff for your occupation? Don't guess. Find out. Show that you have the specific skills employers are looking for. Here's how—

Let's take it from the beginning.

I'm sure you know that a dental hygienist cleans your teeth. So, let's use that occupation in the following example.

1. Name the job you want.

> *Dental Hygienist*

2. List the requirements of the job.

> *Remove calculus and plaque*
> *Take and develop dental x-rays*
> *Teach patient oral-hygiene strategies*
> *Perform oral and neck screening*
> *Perform documentation and office management activities*

3. Select the first requirement from your list.

> *Remove calculus and plaque, also known as cleanings*

4. Give an example of when you performed it.

> *Cleanings: Averaged 120 cleanings per month*

5. Add details.

> *Cleanings: 120 patients per month. Gentle and trusted, 35% of patients ask for me by name*

6. Repeat steps 3, 4, and 5 for each additional job requirement on your list.

· ·

"Lack of technical skills," is the number-one reason employers have trouble filling job openings

—Manpower

Q. "Where can I find the job requirements for my occupation?"

All you need to do is visit Indeed, Career-builder, and Monster. Then, read a dozen help-wanted advertisements for your occupation.

In each ad, look for a statement like, "The ideal candidate will be able to ..." or "Job duties include ...." That's where the hiring manager tells you exactly what she's looking for.

Now, pick out the 5 or 6 common job requirements that all of the ads seem to want. That's the stuff today's hiring managers are looking for. That's the stuff you want to include in your resume.

Q. "What kind of examples should I give?"

Think about the projects you worked on. Specifically, what was accomplished and the special role you played. That's where your best examples will come from. If you don't have one or two of the key job skills, offer a substitute (see Substitute Skills from the column on the right).

Q. "How much detail should I include?"

Mention the important facts. Keep it simple. Whenever possible, include numbers to describe the volume, size, money, time, effort, or result of what you did. Numbers impress people. They allow us to visualize what was accomplished.

Oh—don't get into the why or how of each project. That's the back-story. Save those interesting details for your job interview.

Now, you try it.

1. Name the job you want

_____

2. List the job requirements

a. _____

b. _____

c. _____

d. _____

e. _____

3. Select the first job requirement from your list above and write it down

_____

_____

4. Give an example of when or how you performed it

_____

_____

_____

5. Add details

_____

_____

_____

_____

Continue on the next page—

SUBSTITUTE SKILLS

If you don't have one of the needed job requirements, offer a substitute. A substitute shows that you have similar knowledge.

Similar knowledge shows that you can learn the requirement quicker than if you had no knowledge of the requirement.

For example, if you don't have the sales experience required for a given job, you might talk about your non-profit fund-raising accomplishments instead.

If you don't have the interior decorating experience needed for a job, show pictures of the decorating projects you created at home.

If you don't have the public speaking experience needed for another job, talk about the PowerPoint presentations you gave in high school or college.

Reach into those other areas of your life to find those substitute skills— military, school, sports, volunteering, hobbies, and home projects.

HERE ARE A FEW EXAMPLES FROM DIFFERENT OCCUPATIONS THAT YOU CAN USE TO HELP TURN YOUR PAST PROJECTS INTO THE "RIGHT STUFF"

Select a requirement
Make sandwiches

Give an example
Made custom sandwiches in a mobile deli

Add details
Made 100s of custom sandwiches during lunch-hour rush in a 2-person mobile deli

Select a requirement
Schedule appointments

Give an example
Scheduled appointments in a dental office

Add details
Scheduled appointments in a 3 dentist office serving 200 patients monthly

Select a requirement
Improve web site quality and usability

Give an example
Re-wrote shopping-cart code to simplify customer experience

Add details
Re-wrote shopping-cart code that reduced customer abandoned orders by 8%

· ·

Select a 2nd requirement from your list on page 19

_____

_____

Give an example of when or how you performed it

_____

_____

_____

Add details

_____

_____

_____

_____

_____

Select a 3rd requirement from your list

_____

_____

Give an example of when or how you performed it

_____

_____

_____

Add details

_____

_____

_____

_____

_____

Select a requirement
Supervise personnel

Give an example
Supervised tech support team

Add details
Supervised tech-support team of 7 people who resolved about 900 cases a month

Select a requirement
Train and coach

Give an example
Trained and coached a military squad

Add details
Trained and coached a military squad to provide life-saving emergency-medical treatment in combat: gunshot wounds, explosives, bone fractures, burns, more

Select a requirement
Assist with accounts payable and accounts receivable

Give an example
Asisted bookkeeper with AP and AR for a retail store

Add details
Assisted bookkeeper with AP and AR for a retail store with over 500 accounts and annual sales of $2 million.

· ·

Select a **4th** requirement from your list

_____

_____

Give an example of when or how you performed it

_____

_____

_____

Add details

_____

_____

_____

_____

_____

Select the **5th** requirement from your list

_____

_____

Give an example of when or how you performed it

_____

_____

_____

Add details

_____

_____

_____

_____

_____

Congratulations!

You just turned the job requirements into your accomplishments. Accomplishments impress employers. They show that you are the kind of person who delivers results.

Use the "right stuff" to build a powerful resume

Looking for a job? Then, you need a resume. Your resume is your calling card, your advertisement, your brochure, your flyer. It's a one-page handout that shows what a great catch you are.

Q. "What can I do with a resume?"

Mail it. Email it. Post it online. Ask friends to give it to their managers. Hand it out at job fairs. Give it to employment agencies.

The idea is to get it into the hands of as many hiring managers as you can. If a hiring manager likes what she sees in your resume, you could get invited to a job interview.

Q. "What if I'm not a good writer?"

That's okay. Writing your resume is easy. You completed all the heavy thinking in the last chapter. All that's left to do is type it up.

Q. "Is there some official format or design for a resume?"

No. There is no official format for writing your resume. You can set up your resume any way you like. Feel free to change, modify, expand, ignore, or simplify any of the following suggestions. But, most people do include the following topics in their resumes—

1. Your contact information

Tell employers who you are and how they can reach you.

At the top of the page, type your full name, mailing address, telephone number with area code, plus your text or email address.

Seventy-five percent of hiring managers said they prefer a chronological resume that lists your most recent job first.

—Career Journal

2. Your goal

In one short sentence, tell what kind of work you want.

- "Seeking full-time position as a dragon slayer."

- If you're switching careers and have little experience, say that you are: "Seeking a full-time, junior position as a dragon slayer."

3. Your education

Start with your most recent school or program.

- On the first line in this section, name the award, certification, or degree earned plus the date of the award. If you haven't graduated, simply give the number of credits earned toward the award (36 credits earned toward a BS degree in magic).

- On the second line, give the school's name and city/state address.

- On the third line, list any classes or activities you participated in that would help you in the job you want.

- Repeat for additional schools.

4. Work experience

Start with your most recent employer.

- On the first line in this section, give your job title plus your beginning and ending dates of employment. If you are still employed there, give your starting date and the word "Present" to show that you still hold that job.

- On the next line, give the employer's name and city/state address.

- On the next few lines, list the job requirements with examples from your past (see your notes on pages 19 through 21).

- Repeat for additional employers.

5. Your skills list

Create a section called "Skills."

Then, simply list the names of any important tools, devices, programs, procedures, skills, licenses, and systems that you can operate or perform.

6. Additional information

Create a section called "Additional Information."

You don't have to include this section in your resume. It's optional. But, it is a great place to mention any special talents, skills, abilities or awards that might interest an employer.

• •

On the next page, you'll find a resume that you can use to model your resume on.

Notice how simple and clean it looks. Bold headings, short sentences, and plenty of white space help the requirements jump off the page. Plus, each job requirement is phrased as an accomplishment with an example of what the writer did and numbers to show the size of the projects.

Creating your resume is even easier than you think. Just use the fill-in-the-blank worksheet on page 25.

WHY YOU NEED A SKILLS LIST IN YOUR RESUME

Having a skills section in your resume can be important. Many large employers download the resumes they receive into a database. A database is a computer file that can hold millions of resumes and job applications.

Databases are searchable. That means, if a hiring manager searches her database for "Final Cut" or "Avid" the computer will pull up only the resumes of people who have that film-editing software in their resumes.

So, if you want the hiring manager's computer to pull up your resume, help it find you by including the names of all the important tools, programs, and systems you can operate or perform.

USE ACTION WORDS

Certain words evoke confidence and authority. When offering examples of past job requirements, be sure to start each sentence with an action word, like:

Achieved…
Assembled…
Assisted…
Built…
Cleaned…
Completed…
Convinced…
Created…
Delivered…
Designed…
Developed…
Equipped…
Established…
Experienced…
Guided…
Handled…
Learned…
Led…
Maintained…
Managed…
Operated…
Organized…
Performed…
Planned…
Produced…
Programmed…
Reduced…
Repaired…
Served…
Set up…
Sold…
Supervised…
Taught…
Trained…
Wrote…

A sample resume

Bea Hopeful
4 Hereiam Drive, Mytown, US 11111
Cell/Text: (222) 333-4444

GOAL

Seeking full-time position as a commercial photographer

EDUCATION

Associate's Degree, 06/2010
Shutterbug School of Photography, Cornea Vista, US
Classes included Photoshop, Lighting, Portraiture, Rights/Licensing

Diploma, 06/2007
Aperture High School, F-Stop, US
Contributed 72 images for yearbook, including candid and action shots

WORK EXPERIENCE

Photographer, 08/2010 to present
Sour Pickles Corporation, Puckerville, US 12345

- *Web site:* Assisted marketing department in the creation of web site. Contributed 8 photos for mood-setting home page plus 57 product selections

- *Product Catalog:* Suggested a new photo-design format that increased telephone orders by 5% in 30 days. Catalog is revised quarterly, 48 pages, 57 product items

- *Packaging:* Developed 6 photo concepts for a new-product packaging campaign. The selected prototype sold 40,000 units

- *News Stories:* Contributed public-relations photographs for news stories printed in 7 major trade magazines and 2 national newspapers

- *Employee Recognition:* Created "People at Work" exhibit containing 24 life-sized photos of employees at work, displayed in the corporate lobby, updated monthly

Photographer's Assistant, 08/2007 to 06/2010
Hot Mustard Inc., Condiments, US 67890
Prepared sets, props, and lighting for catalog and advertising photo shoots

SKILLS

Mamiya, Hasselblad, Nikon, Canon, natural light, lightbox, flash, strobe, product staging, Photoshop, Aperture, InDesign, Quark, Wordpress, Dreamweaver, Mac and PC

ADDITIONAL

- Enjoy creative brainstorming with technical, editorial, and marketing teams
- Friendly, enthusiastic, good sense of humor

Worksheet

Your full name
Your address, city, state, zip code
Your cell, text. or email

GOAL

Give the job you are seeking

_____

EDUCATION

Give your diploma or degree and the date of award

_____

Give the school's name and city/state address

_____

· List several courses you took

_____

Repeat for additional schools or training

WORK HISTORY

Give your job title with beginning and ending dates

_____

Give your employer's name and city/state address

_____

· Give a job requirement, with an example

_____

· Give another job requirement, with an example

_____

· Give another job requirement, with an example

_____

· Give another job requirement, with an example

_____

· Give another job requirement, with an example

_____

Repeat for additional employers

SKILLS

Name the important tools, devices, procedures, programs, systems, and licenses you can operate or perform

_____

ADDITIONAL

Mention any special talents, abilities, or awards

_____

BASIC RESUME WRITING TIPS

· Use standard 8.5" by 11" white paper

· Keep a one-inch margin on all four sides of the page

· Avoid fancy fonts like outline, script, or other difficult-to-read styles

· Keep sentences short and to the point

· Bold or CAPITALIZE important headlines so they stand out

· Single space within sections

· Double space between sections

· Use bullets (·) at the beginning of a list

· Whenever possible, use numbers to show the size, volume, time, money, effort, or result of the projects you worked on

· Proofread for spelling and factual errors

How people get job interviews

The job interview is your chance to sit down, face-to-face, with a hiring manager and convince her that she should hire you instead of someone else. How do you get a job interview? Here are some tips.

Employee referrals

Make a list of all the people you know who work in the same field or occupation as you.

Reach out to them. Ask if they could help you get a job interview where they work.

This is called networking—people connecting through other people. You are more likely to be hired if you have an employee connection.

In fact, most employers prefer to hire the friends of their workers. Eighty-eight percent of hiring managers say it's their best source for recruiting above-average candidates. Friends are so valuable, some employers will pay a finder's fee to an employee who brings in a new hire.

As the friend of an employee, you'll also have a special advantage over an outsider. Your inside friend can tell you about the hiring manager—

her interviewing style, her management style, the issues she is most concerned about, the type of person she wants for the job, questions she is likely to ask, and the best way for you to ask for the job.

And here's an added bonus: Unlike answering a help-wanted ad or a job posting, where dozens of people might compete for the job, it's not uncommon for friends to be hired with little or no competition at all.

How to get started:

Call a friend. "Hi, Betty. It's Duncan."

Ask for some help. "I'd like to apply for a job as a baker at Bundt. I know that you work at Bundt. On the job application, it asks if I know someone who works there. Would you mind if I mentioned, that you and I are friends?"

Ask for information about the hiring manager. "Who is the bakery manager at Bundt? Is she

Three sources account for 76% of all new job hires
- Employee referrals create 39.9%
- Employer career sites create 21.2%
- Job boards create 14.6%

—Jobvite Index

the person I should send my resume to? What's she like?"

Ask for a special favor. "Could I ask a favor? Would you mind giving my resume to Ms. Pillsbury and putting in a good word for me?"

Show your gratitude. "Betty, thank you so much. If I get a job interview, I'll bake you a dozen dinner rolls."

Then, reach out to all your other friends too

Use email and social media to connect with them.

Keep your message simple. Explain what you want. "Looking for a job as a coffee taster. Do you know anyone who works in the coffee roasting business?"

Wait for someone to respond. "Maxwell, thanks for answering my message!"

Ask for information. "Maxwell, you said your cousin is the tasting supervisor at Folger's Beanery. Is she the one I should send my resume to? What's she like?

"Could I ask a favor? Would you give her my resume and put in a good word for me?"

Thank your friend. "Thanks so much Maxwell. I'll email my resume to you right now."

Spread the word even further. Always ask your friends if they would forward your message to their friends. Think about it, if your 30 friends talked to their 30 friends, you could have 900 people sending you tips, referrals, and introductions.

Employer career site

Do you have a list of favorite employers? Visit their web sites and see what kind of job openings they have.

How to get started:

Start with your favorite employer. Visit their web site and navigate to their employment page or career page.

Look through the job postings. Apply only for the jobs you are qualified to do. When you find a job that interests you, bookmark that web page so you can find your way back to it later.

Next, contact your friends. Ask if they know any mutual friends who work inside that company. Dig. You are 50 times more likely to get a job if you know an insider.

When you find an inside friend, ask if you could list him as a friend on your job application.

Then, ask a favor. Ask if he would give a copy of your resume to the hiring manager and put in a good word for you.

Be sure to thank your friend for his help and friendship.

Then, move on to the next employer on your favorite's list and repeat the process.

Job boards

Job boards like CareerBuilder, Monster, and CraigsList, plus job-search engines like Indeed and SimplyHired are very popular ways to find job openings.

But don't stop there—check your area's online newspapers for help-wanted ads, plus the help ads posted on Twitter, Facebook, and LinkedIn too.

How to get started:

Submit a clean job application. Don't let misspellings, wrong numbers, missing information, and information typed in the

CREATE A SIMPLE JOB-HUNTING PLAN

Every employer is not hiring today. You have to knock on a lot of doors to find the ones that are. Here's a simple plan that takes only an hour or two a day. Give it a try and see how many interviews you can get.

· Monday through Friday, contact five employers every day. That's 25 employers a week, 100 a month. To reach them, use a good mix of all the ideas in this chapter.

· Now, you may not get a job interview the first week or so because it takes time for employers to respond.

· But, after two weeks, your phone should start to ring.

· When you begin to get job interviews, don't stop contacting five new employers every day. Stick with your plan right up until the day you accept a job offer.

· If you do stop, your flow of interviews will dry up in about two weeks. Then it will take you two more weeks to get the pipeline flowing again.

wrong spaces disqualify you.

To boost your chances of getting a job interview, attach your resume and a cover letter with your job application. Your resume and cover letter offer a lot of information not asked in the job application. Writing a cover letter is fast and easy with AIDA—see the details on page 30.

Walk-ins

One of the easiest ways to get a job interview is to look for "Now Hiring" signs on business buildings, doorways, and billboards.

How to get started:

Walk into the shop, store, or office. Smile, and ask one of the employees if you can fill out a job application. You might say, "Hi, I saw your now-hiring sign. May I have a job application, please?"

Then, ask a few questions to show your interest. You might simply ask, "Which jobs are available? What are the duties of a yodeler? Which days and hours are available?"

Try to get an inside referral. The best way to get a job is to get someone who works inside the company to put in a good word for you. So, while you're in the office, ask the employee if someone from your neighborhood, school, or former employer works there.

If you know the insider, call him when you get home. Mention that you applied for a job where he works. Ask if he could give your resume to the hiring manager and put in a good word for you.

If you don't know any insiders, contact your friends and relatives. See if they know an insider who might be able to help.

Job fairs and open-houses

Where can you meet dozens of recruiters, face to face, all in one day, all in one place? Simple. Go to a job fair or a company open house. Recruiters are standing there, waiting to meet you.

Keep in mind that recruiters do not usually hire people at career fairs. The fair or open-house is an opportunity for them to meet job hunters, collect resumes, and schedule job interviews. They prefer not to interview at the job fair because the fairs are noisy, fast paced, and there are too many people to interview. So they usually schedule interviews which take place a few days after the fair.

To find an event in your area, Google Job Fair, Career Fair, and Company Open House. Also, check for open-house announcements in the help-wanted section of your Sunday newspapers. Oh, and check with your local American Job Center to see if they're planning a job fair or an employers' open house (see page 29).

How to get started:

Once you are inside the job fair, walk up to the employer's table or booth.

Make eye contact with the recruiter, smile, and say hello. Offer your handshake and introduce yourself.

Deliver your "sales pitch" from page 29.

Answer the recruiter's questions.

Offer the recruiter a copy of your resume.

Ask for the recruiter's business card.

Ask how you can schedule a job interview.

Thank the recruiter for speaking with you, smile, and offer your handshake.

When you get home, reintroduce yourself by

sending the recruiter a thank-you note and another copy of your resume. Use the cover letter template on page 31. The thank-you note tells the recruiter that you do want an interview and you took the time to follow-up and ask for one. All of the recruiter's contact information is on her business card—which you picked up at the job fair.

Temporary employment agency

Temporary employment agencies are match makers. They bring together employers that need help and job hunters who need work.

Working for a temp agency is a great way to get your foot in the door at a good company. You'll learn new skills, gain experience, make contacts, and build references. Every year, about 9 million people find work through employment agencies—and 79 percent are placed in full-time positions.

How to get started:

Google "Employment Agencies" for a list of agencies in your area. You might also ask your friends if they've ever worked with an employment agency. Maybe a friend can recommend a good agency for you.

Call the agency and ask to register for employment. The agent will ask a few questions about your background and skills. If you are a good fit for the agency, the agent will ask you to come in for a meeting.

During the meeting, the agent will go over your resume and ask questions about your skills and abilities. For some occupations, like secretarial or graphic design, the agent may ask you to take a skills test to measure your abilities.

The agent will also ask about your needs. Do you want to work for a large company or a small one? How far are you willing to commute? Do you want full-time, part-time, or seasonal work? What wage or salary do you expect?

The agent will then try to match you to a job opening at one of their employer clients.

American Job Centers

The six activities we just discussed are do-it-yourself projects. You can use them to get job interviews, by yourself.

But what if you'd like some help? What if you'd like to talk to someone who can explain the local job market, tell you who the major employers are, look over your resume, and offer some advice on creating a job-hunting plan?

Well, employment counselors are available—and their services are free. Your state government operates a number of American Job Centers. In addition to employment counseling, they also offer job search workshops, use of computers with internet, job fairs and employer open houses, referrals to job training programs, special services for Veterans, and a whole lot more.

Now, lots of employers are very loyal to local Job Centers and like to recruit new employees there. This means that Job Centers have good working relationships with recruiters, hiring managers, and business owners. This relationship can help open the door to a job interview for you.

How to get started:

Call or visit your local Job Center and ask to speak with an employment counselor. Explain what kind of work you're looking for. Ask if the counselor could give you a few referrals—the names of recruiters, hiring managers, or business owners who hire people with your skills.

Once you have their names, send a letter or an email, plus your resume, to introduce yourself to each person. Use the cover letter format on page 24. Then follow-up with a phone call to see if they received your letter and ask for a job interview.

You can find your local Job Center by Googling *American Job Centers* or *One-Stop Career Centers*

CREATE A 15 SECOND SALES PITCH

A sales pitch is a short speech. It's a 15 second "sound bite" that sells you to hiring managers and anyone who can help you get a job interview.

A good sales pitch includes you name, your occupation, your accomplishments, your goal, and your UPS (Unique Selling Point). Your UPS is what separates you from the competition.

Spend some time thinking about your sales pitch. Here's a good example to go by.

"Hi, my name is Mason Stone."

"I've been an apprentice stone mason for the past year and I've learned both wet and dry masonry."

"I've built walkways, terraces, retaining walls, and patios for residential customers. They've been very happy with my work."

"Now, I'm looking for a full-time junior masonry job."

"Let me also add that—I'm a hard worker and I give more than a minimum effort. I'm reliable and I'll show up on time every day. I'm a quick learner and I'm easy to coach. I also have a good sense of humor and I get along with people. I would love to interview with your company."

How to write a better cover letter

A cover letter is a personal letter that you send with your resume or job application. It's the first thing the hiring manager sees when she opens your envelope or email. It's your hello, your smile, your chance to create a rapport, your reason for writing.

Q. "Does everyone send a cover letter with their resume or job application?"

No. Most people don't include a cover letter. And that's why you should send one. It shows that you're different. It shows that you are serious about the job and you cared enough to write.

Q. "Do I have to create a new letter each time I apply to a different company?"

Yes and no. You certainly want all employers to feel that you are writing to them personally. But, you can recycle paragraphs and include them in most of your letters.

Q. "Who should I address my letter to?"

This is important—the hiring manager is usually the manager of the department where you want to work. If you want a job in human resources, send your letter to the human-resource manager. If you want to work in maintenance, send you letter to the maintenance manager. At a small business, send your letter to the owner of the business.

Q. "How do I get the manager's name?"

If you are getting a referral from a friend, ask your friend for the hiring manager's name. When writing, address your letter and envelope to that manager by name and title. For example: Ms. Iva Joboffer, IT Manager. Make sure the manager's name, title, and address are accurate and spelled correctly.

If you are writing to a company and you don't know the manager's name, call the company and ask for it. The receptionist who answers your call will be glad to give you the information you need.

If you are answering an advertisement or job posting that gives no contact person's name or no company name, address your letter to *Hiring Manager*.

Eighty-six percent of executives said cover letters are important when evaluating job candidates.

—National Association of Workforce Development Professionals

Q. "How long does my cover letter have to be?"

Keep your cover letter short and simple. One page is perfect.

Q. "Could you help me write my letter?"

You bet. But first, I'd like you to meet AIDA.

Q. "Who's AIDA?"

The folks who write professional sales letters use a magic formula. It's called AIDA. That's short for—Attention, Interest, Desire, Action.

AIDA sells billions of dollars worth of goods and services every year. If it can work for business, it can work for you. So, let's use AIDA to convince a hiring manager to give you a job interview.

1. Attention

In the very first paragraph of your letter, grab the hiring manager's attention simply by telling her why you are writing. Below are several solid reasons for writing to a hiring manager. Adapt the ONE that works best for you.

- "I would like to apply for the sous chef's position I saw advertised in..."
- "My friend, Frieda Friendly works in your department. She recommended that I write to you."
- "We spoke at a career fair last..."
- "I stumbled upon your website. Wow. I'd like to interview for a position with your firm because..."
- "I shop at your store and..."
- "I would like to learn about the career opportunities for mechanics at your shop."

2. Interest

In the second paragraph of your letter, rouse the manager's interest by explaining what makes you special. Here are a few examples. Adapt the ONE that works best for you.

- "I have three-years experience as a..."
- "I worked on the Slingshot project at David's and..."
- "I just graduated from school and..."
- "I have three special abilities I can bring to the job..."
- "I have an idea I'd like to discuss with you..."

3. Desire

If you are responding to a help-wanted advertisement or a job posting, be sure to talk about the job requirements the ad says are important. Otherwise, create a desire for the hiring manager to meet you by offering three solid accomplishments.

- "I am very familiar with..."
- "I know how to use..."
- "I also have experience with..."

4. Action

Finally, ask the hiring manager for a job interview. Adapt ONE of the following statements that works best for you.

- "I would like to interview for your nursing position. Please call. You can reach me anytime on my cell phone at 555-666-7777."
- "I would like to interview for your nursing position. I hope you won't mind if I call in a few days to see that you received my resume and hopefully to schedule an interview."

WHEN RESPONDING BY EMAIL

Some help-wanted advertisements will ask you to email your resume and a cover letter to the employer.

Here are a few general tips. But, always follow the advertisement's instructions.

If the advertisement gives you a contact person's name like Ms. Smith or a job code number, type it in the "Subject" box of the email. This will ensure that your email gets routed to the proper hiring manager within the company.

If the advertisement does not include a contact person's name or a job code, type the advertisement's job title, *Carnival Barkers' Job,* in the email's "Subject" box.

Unless the employer tells you otherwise, copy and paste your letter into the body of your email. Include your resume as an attachment.

You may be asked to send your attached resume as a Microsoft Word document, a text file, or as a PDF.

To create a text file or PDF in Microsoft Word, go to: File > Save As > Format > Plain Text or PDF.

A sample letter using AIDA

▶
Your name and contact information

Pat Perfect
One Pluperfect Way
Anytown, US 12345
(111) 222-3333
pat@email.com

Date ▶

December 31, 20XX

▶
Hiring manager's name and address

Ms. Karin K. Boom, Owner
New Day Demolitions, Inc.
55 Nowhiring Highway
Anytown, US 12345

Job Code ▶

Re: Job Code 5678, from the *Blabbermouth*

Salutation ▶

Dear Ms. Boom:

Attention ▶

I would like to apply for your Office Receptionist's position, which I saw advertised in Wednesday's edition of the *Blabbermouth.*

Interest ▶

Ms. Boom, I can offer you three years of experience as a receptionist. I have a cheerful helpful personality, and I have a good memory for names, faces, voices, and telephone numbers.

Desire ▶

· I am familiar with most telephone systems, fax machines, email, plus both Apple and Microsoft operating systems.

· I have hands-on experience with QuickBooks, Microsoft Word, Excel, and appointment scheduling software.

· I also have experience as a bill collector. If the need arises, I would be happy to make collection calls or field difficult or awkward inquiries.

Action ▶

I would love to interview for this position. I hope you'll call. You can reach me anytime on my cell at (111) 222-3333.

When you do call, please understand that the child's voice on my voice-mail greeting is not my voice!

I look forward to your call.

Closing ▶

Sincerely,

Signature ▶

Pat Perfect

Printed name ▶

Pat Perfect

Worksheet

Your name
Your address
Your city, state, zip
Your phone number
Your email address

Today's date

Manager's name and title
Department's name
Company's name
Address
City, state, zip

Re: (Job code, if listed in an ad or job posting)

Dear (Mr. or Ms.):

(Get the manager's attention)

_____

_____

(Rouse the manager's interest)

_____

_____

(Create a desire to meet you)

· _____

· _____

· _____

(Ask the manager to take action)

_____

_____

Sincerely,

Your Signature

Pat Perfect

Prepare for the hiring manager's phone call

You've found a job opening and applied for the position. Now, if the hiring manager likes what she sees in your resume, she'll give you a call. Don't underestimate the importance of this phone call. It's actually a screening interview. The purpose of the call is to decide whether to invite you to a face-to-face job interview. Here are five tips to help you pass the screen and win an invitation to the interview.

1. Have a professional greeting

You never know when an employer might call, so answer every phone call with a professional greeting. Sure, your friends will laugh when they call and hear you say, "Hello. This is Ken Dooit. How can I help you?" But the hiring managers will love it.

Also, record a new phone message. Something short and professional like this—"Hello. This is Ken Dooit. I'm not able to answer the phone. Please leave your name, phone number, and a brief message. I do check my messages often. I'll return your call as soon as possible. Thank you."

2. When they call, most hiring managers will ask if this is a convenient time to speak with you.

Managers know that you have a life. If you're at work, driving your car, or sitting in the dentist's chair, it's okay to arrange another time to talk.

When you return a call, choose a place where you'll be free from noise, interruptions, and where your cell phone has good reception.

You might say—

"Good afternoon, Ms. Hireyou. My name is Ken Dooit. I'm returning your phone call. I applied for a job as a tight-rope walker."

3. Don't wing it

Prepare and rehearse like this is a real interview. Because it is. If you bomb this screening interview, you won't get the face-to-face interview or the job offer.

So, be prepared. Have your resume, cover letter, job advertisement, and notes from the employer's website in front of you.

You can't know which questions a hiring

Your telephone conversation with a hiring manager could last between ten minutes and an hour.

—*Wall Street Journal*

manager might ask, so look over these common questions plus those on page 44.

- Are you currently employed? Where?
- What is your job title?
- How long have you been working there?
- What are your duties and responsibilities?
- Tell me about your job skills.
- Do you get along with your supervisor?
- Why are you leaving?
- When are you available to begin work?
- Why do you want to work for my company?
- What motivates you to do a good job?
- What are your career goals?

4. Relax

Try to visualize what the manager looks like based on the sound of his or her voice—maybe a favorite cousin, friend, or teacher. This will help make the manager seem more familiar and less intimidating.

Don't forget to smile—even on the phone. Smiling helps project a personality that comes across in your voice. You should also stand up while speaking on the phone and use your hands to gesture. Thinking on your feet and gesturing helps with your thought processes. They'll also help slow down your speech so you don't slur your words and start to spit.

5. Watch your manners

Always refer to the manager as Mr. or Ms., unless the hiring manager asks you to use their first name. Be sure to say please and thank you.

Don't sip a drink, chew gum, or nibble on food, the manager will hear it and it's rude.

Don't use foul or inappropriate language—this is the workplace not the schoolyard.

Try not to say, "No problem," "Uh-huh," "Like," or "Ya know," too often. They can become annoying.

Also, don't ask about money, benefits, or vacations—they are usually discussed when a job offer is made.

Be willing to accept the hiring manager's interview schedule, even if you have to reschedule the cable guy.

Confirm the date and time of the interview by repeating it back to the hiring manager—"That's Thursday the 13th at 3:13…"

Thank the hiring manager for showing an interest in you—"Ms. Hireyou, thank you so much for this opportunity. I look forward to meeting you on Thursday. Bye."

And here's a big one. Don't take another phone call or try to read your text messages during this phone interview. It's the #1 reason a hiring manager will hang up on you. So, turn off the dings and rings before your phone interview begins. Let the manager feel that she is your most important phone call.

Okay, one more tip

If the manager doesn't offer you a job interview, ask for one. That's what this phone call is all about. You might say something as simple as this—"I'm very interested in this position. I would love to visit your company. Could we schedule an interview?"

DON'T LET YOUR SOCIAL-MEDIA SITES KEEP AN EMPLOYER FROM CALLING YOU

A CareerBuilder/Harris Poll reports that most hiring managers will Google a job applicant's name to see if he or she has a social media presence on Facebook, LinkedIn, Twitter, and other sites.

Hiring managers aren't looking for negative information. They simply want to get a read on a job applicant's personality and hear what other people have to say about them.

A friendly and helpful online personality, a professional image, good communication skills, and a little creativity will make a very nice impression.

However, inappropriate photographs, information about drinking or drug use, bad-mouthing a previous employer or coworker, vile language, and negative comments about race, religion, or gender are real turn-offs.

Some hiring managers will even ask to friend or follow the job applicant. This can open the door to the job applicant's private pages. So, be careful what you allow people to see on your social media pages—it can affect whether a hiring manager chooses to call you or not.

Find three people who will give you a "positive recommendation"

You are a good worker. You give more than the minimum. You show up everyday and you're never late. You're easy going and everybody likes you. Well, that's great but the hiring manager wants proof. She wants to talk to three people who can vouch for you.

Q. "Who should I include as references?"

Most hiring managers want three reliable references. Ideally, they want the name of your current boss—but NOT if that boss doesn't know that you're looking for another job. In that case, they'll want the name of your previous employer.

Other good references might include former supervisors, coworkers, customers, teachers, coaches, and prominent people who know you. Prominent people might include an attorney, a banker, a doctor, a member of the clergy, or a local business owner.

Q. "Am I supposed to ask before offering someone's name as a job reference?"

Yes. Always ask. People who agree to serve as references almost always give a better recommendation than those who are not asked.

Those who are NOT asked are often caught off guard. They might struggle to remember who you are, what you did, and when you worked for them. To a hiring manager this hesitation might sound like your reference is not eager to recommend you.

Q. "How do I ask someone to be a reference? What do I say?"

Call or visit them. Don't ask by text or email. You need to see each person's face or hear their voice when you ask.

80%

Eighty percent of employers said they regularly conduct reference checks.

—The Society for Human Resource Management

When you do ask, don't just ask for a recommendation. Ask for a "positive recommendation."

You might say, "Elmer, I'm applying for work as a ballerina. I would like to list you as a reference. Would you be able to give me a positive recommendation?"

Most people are flattered when asked. They'll be happy to give you a good recommendation and they'll say so.

Others might not be interested in singing your praises. So, listen to their voice. Notice their body language. What does your gut tell you? If you don't think they'll give you a good recommendation, don't use them.

Q. "I know my former boss won't give me a good recommendation. Do I have to list him as a reference?"

Could you ask your boss's boss for a recommendation instead?

Q. "Maybe I should just tell the hiring manager that my boss and I didn't get along."

The manager will admire your honesty.

Here's a big tip—never badmouth a former boss. It screams that you are a troublemaker.

Instead, put a positive spin on a negative situation. Try this: "Mr. Pumpernickel was the most demanding boss I ever worked for. We had our moments. But, I learned more from him than anyone I've ever worked for. I'll probably miss him."

Q. "Should I list my references on my resume?"

No. Your resume will pass through lots of hands— friends, friends-of-friends, and probably a few people you might not even know. You don't want the names of your references to fall into the wrong hands. So, keep them off your resume. Another thing, if you put your references on your resume, you are inviting hiring managers to call your references before they've even met you.

Instead, list your references on a separate sheet of paper. Include each person's name, address, phone number, employer, job title, and best times for the hiring manager to call. Hand your list of references to the hiring manager during your job interview.

Q. "Should I send my references a copy of my resume?"

Yes. Don't let them struggle to remember who you are and what you did on the job.

Once someone agrees to give you a positive reference, refresh his or her memory of you. Send a copy of your resume plus a list of the projects or assignments you worked on together. Be sure to include your duties, responsibilities, accomplishments and any other information that might help them write a good recommendation for you.

QUESTIONS A HIRING MANAGER MIGHT ASK YOUR REFERENCES

- Were you Heidi Hopeful's immediate supervisor?
- What was Heidi's job title?
- What were her dates of employment?
- What was her salary?
- What were her duties and responsibilities?
- What were her most significant accomplishments?
- Did Heidi receive any promotions or awards?
- What was Heidi's attitude toward work?
- What was her level of energy at work?
- Did she get along with her coworkers and managers?
- How often was she late or absent?
- What were her job strengths?
- In which skills does Heidi need improvement?
- Why did Heidi leave the job?
- If possible, would you rehire her?
- Is there anything I didn't ask you, that I should have asked?

Enthusiasm, the key to a great interview

Hiring managers agree—enthusiasm separates the winners from the losers. It can be more important than experience. "Give me someone who's enthusiastic and motivated," explained one manager, "someone who's alert and alive... someone who's interested in what we do here... someone who's excited about coming to work for me... someone who wants to help me as much as I want to help them."

You don't need to be one of those loud, back-slapping types

Just be you.

Dress like you belong there

Wear the clothes that you would wear on the job. If you're not sure what to wear, call the company and ask someone in their human resource department. They'll be glad to help.

Plan to arrive ten-minutes early for your interview

It shows that you are excited to be there. Hiring managers are clock watchers. They'll notice.

Be extra courteous

Say hello, smile, and be friendly to everyone you meet. You can bet that the manager will ask what they thought of you, after you've left the building.

Offer a professional greeting

When you meet the manager, stand up straight, look her in the eye, smile, extend a firm handshake, and say, "Ms. Joboffer, thank you so much for taking the time to interview me for your (cat herding) position."

About that handshake

Engage the full hand, palm to palm. Grip firmly to show that you mean it, but don't crush.

Don't undersell yourself and don't oversell yourself. Sales people who are middle-verts outsell introverts by 29 percent and outsell extraverts by 24 percent.

—The Wharton School, University of Pennsylvania

Look the other person in the eye. Smile. Pump two or three times. Release.

Show respect for the manager's position

Address the manager as Mr. or Ms., unless they ask you to call them by their first name. Once you're in the manager's office, don't sit down until you're invited to sit. Be sure to look at the manager whenever she speaks.

Show some curiosity

Ask for a short tour of the workplace before the interview begins. Look around. Ask questions about the cool things you see. Talk shop—ask what the manager thinks of the latest software, the newest gadget, or the hot new trend in your industry.

Have a sense of humor

We are drawn to happy, optimistic, humorous people. When appropriate, offer a clever quip, a one-liner, or an interesting tale. Keep it short, positive and upbeat. Don't forget to chuckle at the manager's attempts at humor.

Think, "can do"

If a manager says you don't have a certain skill or enough experience, don't just shrug your shoulders. Most managers want to see whether you'll fight for what you want or whether you'll just give up.

So, tell the hiring manager that you're a quick learner, a hard worker, and that you always deliver more than what's expected. Let her know that you will become one of the best employees she will ever hire.

Let your body language do some talking

Sit up straight. Sit near the edge of the chair with both feet on the floor. Visualize your ideas and use your hands to illustrate what you mean. Look the manager in the eye. Use facial expressions to emphasize important points.

Show a little empathy

Empathy means that you understand how the other person feels. When the manager talks about an important issue, look at her eyes to show that you are listening, use facial expressions to show that you understand, and ask for details to show that you care.

Have a reason for wanting to work there

Visit the company's website and Google the company name for news. Find out who they are, what they do, and why you want to work there.

Participate in the conversation

The interview should be a 50/50 conversation. Don't be a motor-mouth who never stops talking. And don't be a zombie who hardly says a word. Listen. Ask questions. Give generous answers.

Become a storyteller

You probably have a great reason for choosing your line of work. When the manager asks, "What made you decide to become a puppeteer?"—tell your story. Include lots of detail and use body language to bring your story to life.

TRY A LITTLE MIRRORING

Mirroring is a body-language dance where you copy the hiring manager's actions. It creates a bond. It says, "we're in sync."

Mirroring is not new. Everybody does it. If you smile at someone, they'll usually smile back. Like the smile, most mirroring is unintentional. But, if you are aware of mirroring, you can boost its effectiveness.

Here are some simple mirroring tips:

- When the hiring manager smiles or frowns, you should smile or frown too.
- If the manager uses hand gestures to add emphasis, you should use hand gestures when you want to add emphasis.
- If the manager sits up straight or leans toward you, you should sit straight or lean too.
- If the manager speaks quickly or slowly, you should match her pace when speaking.
- If the manager uses special job-related words or technical terms, you should use them too.

Navigate your way through a job interview

Managers are expert interviewers and they know that you're going to be nervous. To help you relax and feel comfortable, they'll conduct the interview as if it were a casual, friendly conversation. Now, each manager has her own style and personality. There is no set format to a job interview. But there is a beginning, a middle, and an end. So, let's walk through the interview from beginning to end and see how it unfolds.

Your arrival

Come prepared for each interview. Don't wing it. Visit the company's website. Know who they are, what they do, and have a good reason why you want to work there.

When you first arrive, check in with the receptionist. Smile and introduce yourself. You might say, "Hi, my name is Luke Atmenow. I have a 4:14 appointment with Ms. Ida Hireyou in the imagineering department. When you have a moment could you please let her know that I'm here? Thank you."

If you're wearing a winter coat or a raincoat, ask where you can hang your coat. Don't bring it into the interview with you. You'll look awkward carrying it. Plus, carrying a coat gives the impression that this is a quick meeting and you'll be in and out in just a few minutes. Besides, what will you do with it once you're in the hiring manager's office? It's best if you hang your coat in the waiting room.

After checking your coat, visit the rest room. Check your hair, teeth, clothes and turn off your phone. Some hiring managers say they would not hire someone who took a cell call during a job interview.

Oh, while you're in the rest room, try this. Lock your-self into a stall. Then, strike the Superman pose. You know, feet apart, standing tall, hands on your hips, gazing upward. Hold that pose for two full minutes. You could walk into the interview feeling like you could change the world.

The average job interview lasts about 55 minutes. Interviews for management-level positions last about 86 minutes.

—Robert Half Recruitment

Seriously. A Harvard psychologist found that power posing reduced stress and increased confidence by about 20 percent.

Okay. Looking good? Feeling good? Phone turned off? Take a seat in waiting area. Sit up straight. Try not to fidget. Run through the interview in your mind. Visualize the important parts—like an athlete might visualize an upcoming event.

The greeting

The hiring manager will usually come into the waiting area to meet you. Sometimes an assistant will greet you and escort you to hiring manager's office.

Either way, when someone mentions your name, stand up. Smile and say, "Hi, I'm Luke Atmenow." The hiring manager will smile, walk toward you and introduce herself.

Offer your handshake and say, "It's so nice to meet you, Ms. Hireyou. Thank you for inviting me to this interview." Saying her name will help you remember it.

As you are escorted to the hiring manager's office, make small talk to show that you are friendly and sociable.

Big tip: Find something other than the weather or the traffic to chat about. Hiring managers hear the same chatter from dozens of different job hunters every day.

Instead, offer a compliment or a positive observation. You might mention how friendly everyone in the front office was to you, and give an example. You might compliment the handsome building and explain why you like it. Or, better yet, explain why you are so thrilled to be interviewing with this company. Make a good first impression and you'll set the tone for a good interview.

Another tip: If the hiring manager is escorting you to her office, ask for short tour to see the inner workings before the interview starts. Most people won't ask for a tour. If you do, the hiring manager will be impressed that you're interested—and that you asked. Plus, a short tour will give you a chance to establish a rapport with the hiring manager and gain an insight into her personality before the Q&A starts.

The start

Once you're both seated in the hiring manager's office, the manager will lean forward, smile and say, "Okay, tell me a little about yourself."

That's one of the most common opening questions. And, it's the perfect time to deliver your fifteen-second sales pitch from page 29. Your pitch is quick, to point, and it will show the hiring manager, right off, that you have the stuff she's looking for.

When you've finished delivering your pitch, offer the hiring manager your typed list of references. In return, ask for her business card. Asking for her business card is important—her business card will have all the information you'll need to follow-up after the interview is over.

The hiring manager will then take your resume out of her folder, give it a glance, and say, "I see here that you were the Over-and-Under guy at Round & Round. Can you tell me about your duties there?"

Keep in mind that your resume simply lists your accomplishments. It doesn't explain any of the back-story on those accomplishments.

BECOME A STORY TELLER

Instead of explaining how or why you did something, try telling it as a story. Stories bring events to life.

A good story has three main parts, the beginning, middle, and end.

Another way to look at a good story is problem, struggle, outcome.

The problem, struggle, and outcome raise the energy of the story and make it more interesting.

Here's a little format you can use to craft your story.

- *Problem.* "I worked with some very difficult customers. For example..."

- *Struggle.* "I tried... I also tried... Then one day..."

- *Outcome.* "A week later..."

Keep your stories short and simple, about a minute each. Use your hands, facial expressions, and voice to bring them to life. Add a little humor whenever you can.

Stories can help you stand out. Long after you've left the interview, the hiring manager may not remember your name, but she'll remember your interesting story. "Hmmm," she'll think, "Maybe I should call that person who worked with all those difficult customers."

This is your chance to tell those stories. So, count off your main duties and tell how you turned each duty into an accomplishment. Be brief, but tell enough, and don't exaggerate—you don't need to.

The hiring manager will ask for details during your story. Give generous answers. Add a little humor when you can. Use hand gestures and facial expressions to bring your story to life.

If the conversation slows or lulls, weave in some questions of your own to create the ebb and flow of a two-way conversation. You might ask—

- "What are the department's goals for the year?"
- "What are the major challenges the new hire will face in this job?"
- "How long should it take for me to get my feet on the ground and become productive?"
- "Who are the key people I'd be working with and what do they do?"
- "Which employee do you rely upon most? What does she do and what makes her unique?"
- "How would I get feedback on my performance?"
- "How soon do you plan to fill this job?"

One thing, though, don't ask questions about wages, benefits, or vacations. To paraphrase President Kennedy, "Ask not what the company can do for you, show what you can do for the company." Besides, wages and benefits are usually discussed when the job offer is made.

The Q&A

By now you're probably warmed up and feeling a bit more confident. So, the hiring manager will start to ask some probing questions. She'll dig a little deeper into your work projects to measure your skills, personality, and judgement.

There are two types of questions the hiring manager will ask, common and behavioral. Common questions require a simple answer, like, "Can you work weekends?" Behavioral questions require some thought, "What would you do if one manager told you to do something and another manager told you not to do it?"

Hiring managers ask behavioral questions to see how you think, solve problems, and sort things out. There's usually no right or wrong answer.

There are fifty questions on pages 44 and 45 —both common and behavioral. There are also suggestions on how to answer them. Spend some time on those questions. Come up with a good answer for each one. You might write them down on flash cards and quiz yourself. Rehearse with a friend to get the kinks out of your answers, before the interview.

The close

Eventually, the conversation will start to slow down and the hiring manager will ask if you have any final questions. This is a sign that the interview is about to end.

Most of your questions will already be answered. But, you do want one or two solid, final questions up your sleeve. A good final question leaves a good final impression.

Here are three:

- *You might ask a personal question.* "How did you get into the face-painting industry?" This shows the hiring manager that you're interested in other people and that you'll integrate easily into the team.

- *You could ask the manager to give you a thirty-day trial period to prove yourself.* It's a gutsy move that very few job hunters will offer, but it tells the hiring manager that you really want this job—and she'll remember that.

- *You could also ask, "How much autonomy or self-direction would I have on the job?"* This shows that you're responsible, a self-starter, the type of person who gets things done—a rare breed, a good catch.

When the hiring manager stands up, the interview is over. You should also stand. Then, look the hiring manager in the eye, smile, offer your handshake, and thank her for meeting with you.

Now, most job hunters never say whether they want the job or not, so make sure you do. You could simply say, "I'm pleased with what I've learned today. I want this position. Where do we go from here?"

The manager will probably say, "I'm still interviewing other candidates, I'll let you know."

Ask if you could follow up in a week, by phone, to see if she's made a decision

As she walks you to the door, say thanks again and mention that you hope she'll call.

And that's it.

Now, off to the follow-up on page 46.

SO, HOW'D YOU DO IN THERE?

Grade your interview with this easy scoring system:

1 = Needs more work
2 = Just OK— room for improvement
3 = Total win

Did you do your homework and know who the employer is, what they do, and why you want to work there?
1 **2** **3**

Did you know which skills were required for the job and show the manager that you are a good fit for that job?
1 **2** **3**

Did you offer examples to show that you are a hard worker and that you deliver more than the minimum?
1 **2** **3**

Did you answer tough questions without stumbling or getting flustered?
1 **2** **3**

Did you ask questions to learn more about the company and the job?
1 **2** **3**

Did you look the manager in the eye and speak clearly?
1 **2** **3**

Did you wear the proper clothes and look your best?
1 **2** **3**

Did you show enthusiasm, a sense of humor, and a positive attitude?
1 **2** **3**

Were you polite and respectful throughout the interview?
1 **2** **3**

Did you ask for the job?
1 **2** **3**

Add up your score. A perfect score is 30. Work on those areas where you need improvement. Think of every interview as practice for the next one.

50 questions to expect during your job interview

1. "Can you tell me a little about yourself?"
Give your 15-second sales pitch from page 29. After you've given your sales pitch, hand the hiring manager a fresh copy of your resume plus your typed list of references. This is important—ask for the hiring manager's business card. That business card will have all of the manager's contact information, including her email address and direct phone number. You'll need this information so you can stay in touch with the hiring manager after the interview is over.

2. "Tell me what you know about my company."
Before you go on the interview, be sure to visit the company's website. Get an overview of the company's key products and services. Google the company name for news. Find out who they are, what they do, and why you want to work for them.

3. "Why did you decide to become a (snake charmer)?"
Tell your story. Include lots of detail and use body language to bring your story to life. Add a touch of humor when appropriate.

4. "What skills or requirements do you think are needed for this job?"
Refer back to pages 18 and 19. Use your fingers and count off the job requirements: 1... 2... 3... 4... 5...

5. "What motivates you to do a good job?"
Money is not a good answer. Instead, try this: "Having responsibilities and getting a pat on the back when the job is done right."

6. "Why is customer service so important in business today?"
"Customers who receive helpful service from friendly employees are more apt to come back again and again. They are also more apt to tell their friends about us. Good service means more business."

7. "Why should I hire you instead of someone more qualified?"
Toot your horn. Tell the manager that you have more than good skills to offer— you're a team player, you're not afraid of hard work, you're a quick learner, you're reliable, you give more than just the minimum effort, and—you want to work for this company because...

8. "Did you ever have a disagreement with your boss?"
Answer "yes" and you're a troublemaker, answer "no" and you're a wimp. Find the middle ground: "Sure we disagreed. But we worked well together. For example..."

9. "Tell me about the toughest boss you ever worked for."

20. "What salary were you paid on your last job?"
Tell the truth.

21. "As a youngster, what did you do to earn your own spending money?"
Baby-sitting, lemonade stand, newspaper route, shoveling snow, mowing lawns, and other jobs show early signs of ambition and a respect for work.

22. "What do you do to relax after work?"
Don't brag about auto racing, bungee jumping, chain-saw juggling, or any other sport that might be dangerous. They suggest a likelihood of injury and an absence from work. Instead, mention something wholesome like athletics, a hobby, a project, traveling, or entertaining friends.

23. "Are you at your best when working alone or in a group?"
"Both. I enjoy working as part of a team and I can work independently to get my share of the work done. For example..."

24. "Would you rather be in charge of a project or work as part of the team?"
"Either. I'm not afraid to take responsibility and I'm not afraid to roll up my sleeves and pitch in."

25. "Have you ever been fired from a job?"
Everybody gets fired from a job at least once in their lifetime. And don't be afraid to tell the truth if it was your fault. Fessing up says that you are a responsible, mature adult. Explain what happened. Explain what you learned. Explain what you would do differently if the same situation happened again.

26. "Tell me about your strengths."
From page 18, you know the five or six requirements needed for the job you want. Choose your strongest job requirements and offer examples to show how you excelled.

27. "What are your weaknesses?"
Choose one or two weaknesses that are not part of the job requirements. Be sure to include an action point to show what you did about each weakness. For instance, "I'm terrified of public speaking. I get so nervous I start to shake. So, I signed up for a stand-up comedy class to help get over the jitters."

28. "Tell me about your favorite accomplishment."
A personal touch works well here, such as your marriage, birth of a child, or helping someone in need. You could also offer something both personal and benevolent. "I'm no athlete, but I did run a 5 kilometer road race in under 45 minutes—and I raised over $1,000 in pledges for

36. "If you were told to report to a supervisor who was a woman, a minority, or someone with a physical disability, what problems would this create for you?"
"I don't see any problems. I genuinely like people. I'm easy to coach and I'm easy to work with. For example..."

37. "Tell me, what would you do if one supervisor told you to do something, and another supervisor told you not to do it?
The manager wants to see how you would handle a dilemma. Try this: Think about what would happen if you did act, and what would happen if you did not act. Write down the pros and cons of each. Make a decision.

38. "Tell me about a time when you broke the rules."
Sometimes it's necessary to break the rules. Just make sure your reasoning and judgement are sound.

39. "Can you tell me about a time when a supervisor was not pleased with your work?"
The manager wants to know how you react to criticism. Here are a few tips to keep in mind when preparing your answer: Top employees see criticism as a learning experience, not a reprimand. They listen without arguing or becoming defensive. They learn what needs to be done differently. They agree to the changes and implement them. They follow up by asking the supervisor for a new critique of their work. They also regain their enthusiasm and confidence quickly.

40. "Tell me about a time when you were swamped with work and how you handled it."
The manager wants to know how you prioritize your time. Experts suggest you start by making a list of all the tasks you need to do today. Next, arrange those tasks from most important to least important. Then, select the task which is most urgent. Start there.

41. "Please tell me about a time when you showed initiative at work."
Initiative is not about working harder. Initiative is about doing more than what your job requires. For example: Taking on a new responsibility without being asked, taking a class or reading a book to learn a new skill, or noticing a problem on the horizon and taking action to correct it.

42. "Describe a difficult decision you had to make."
The manager wants to know about your decision-making skills. Here's a basic decision-making formula: Define the problem, learn what others did in similar situations, list the pros and cons for each option, then choose the best option.

43. "Tell me about a time when you failed."

explain what went wrong, and explain the lesson learned from the failure.

10. "What salary or wage are you looking for?"

Get the manager to throw out the first figure. Ask, "What salary or wage do you usually offer someone with my skills and abilities?"

11. "Tell me about your current (or last) job."

Give the company's name and what they do. Give your job title. List your duties and responsibilities. Explain your accomplishments.

12. How did you feel about being laid off?

Don't bad-mouth your old employer. Admit that you miss the job and the people. Say that you are grateful for the opportunities and the skills you learned there.

13. How long have you been looking for a job?

"A few weeks. I wanted to spend some time with my family. Now I'm ready to get back to work."

14. "Did you enjoy school?"

The manager wants to know if you enjoy learning and whether you might benefit from a training program.

15. "In school, which course did you find most difficult?"

The manager wants to know if you have perseverance: "My first term in history, I got a D. My study skills were all wrong, so I joined a study group. By second term I pulled it up to a B and kept it there."

16. Did you participate in any school activities?

School activities show that you're sociable. They show that you enjoy being part of a group and that you can work with other people. This is important in the work place.

17. "Do you plan to continue your education?"

Adding to your education says that you want to grow and prosper, professionally as well as personally.

18. "What do you hope to get out of this job?"

Try this—"A fair and reasonable wage, responsibility for doing something that matters, a say in how my work is done, recognition by my coworkers for being good at what I do, and a pat on the back from the boss for doing a good job."

19. "Last year, how many days of work (or school) did you miss? How many days were you late?"

This will tell the manager whether you're going to show up for work on time every day. If you've missed more than a few days, have some good explanations ready.

---

and why did you choose them?"

"I chose a good mix—a former boss who can tell you about my skills and job performance—a coworker who can tell you about the hard work and extra effort we put in as a team—and a former coach who can tell you that I'm not only a good team player, I can work independently and I always complete my share of the work."

30. "What are the three things you look for when considering a new job?"

The things that make people happiest at work are not always about money and benefits. Experts say that the following things are often more important: being appreciated, having respect, being trusted, taking on new challenges, having a good boss, working with people you enjoy, and making a difference.

31. "How are you unique?"

Try this: "I'm a quick learner, a hard worker, I'm easy to coach, and I always deliver more than what's expected. I could be one of the best employees you'll ever hire."

▶ The following include some behavioral questions. Behavioral questions help the manager see how you might act or behave in certain situations.

32. "Tell me how you keep a positive attitude when the job gets stressful?"

Here's how positive people stay positive: They know that attitude is a choice. They choose to plan ahead and schedule the time needed to get things done. They choose to be around other positive people. They choose to laugh and have a sense of humor. They choose to be friendly and helpful to everyone. They choose to offset negative thoughts by looking for the positive points.

33. "Please tell me about a time when you had to motivate a coworker."

Some of the best motivational tools include praise and encouragement, giving a helpful demonstration or example, explaining the rewards of the job, and brainstorming for better ways to do the job.

34. "Can you tell me about a goal you set for yourself?"

The manager wants to know if you set goals. People who set goals are more productive than those who do not set goals. The best goals are specific, measurable, and plausible. For example, "I want to pay off my $1,000 car loan in six months," is a better goal than, "I want to pay off my car loan quickly."

35. "Describe a problem you faced and how you solved that problem."

Think of something related to work, school, sports, or volunteering. Tell it as a story. The manager wants to see how you: 1). Define the problem, 2). Identify options and, 3). Decide on a solution.

---

44. "Describe a time when you had to work with a difficult person."

The manager wants to see how you interact with moody, lazy, or obnoxious people. Ideally, you are a peacemaker who tries to resolve conflicts. When provoked, you have a private talk with the person. You remain pleasant. You explain how the behavior makes you feel. And you try to reach an agreement with the culprit.

45. "Please tell me about a time when you were disappointed.

The manager isn't so much interested in what happened, but what you did about that disappointment. Try something like this. "When I didn't get the promotion—I was surprised and hurt. But, I swallowed my pride and congratulated the winner—she earned that promotion. The next day, I reviewed my work performance. I redoubled my efforts, and I haven't missed a promotion since."

46. "Tell me about a project you worked on."

The manager wants to know about your role in the project, specifically what you did. Begin by describing the project and the project's goal. Then, describe the team you worked with, specifically your duties, your responsibilities, your contribution, and any new skills you learned. Finally, tell whether the project met its goals.

47. "Tell me where you expect to be 5 years from now?"

Try this: "It's hard to tell where anyone will be five years from now. But, I am looking for a company where I'll be appreciated, trusted, and able to make a difference. I want to work with people I enjoy, people who challenge me, and a good boss who's not afraid to tell us we did a good job. I think your company might be the one I'm looking for. That's why I'm here today."

48. "Are there any questions I didn't ask, that I should have asked?"

This is a great time to bring up any special skill, ability, or accomplishment that wasn't discussed.

49. "Okay, you've got one minute to convince me that you're the best person for this job. Begin."

Do it in only 30 seconds and you'll make a big impression. Start by delivering your 15-second sales pitch. Then, spend 15 seconds explaining why you want to work for this company. End by asking for the job.

50. "Do you have any questions for me?"

On pages 42 and 43 you'll find a list of questions to ask the hiring manager. Add a few questions of your own to the list.

Surviving A Layoff, © Copyright, Harry Dahlstrom

The art of the follow-up

When you get home from your interview, send the manager a thank-you note. Two days later, send the manager an *idea* note. A week after your interview, pick up the phone and give the manager a call. Then, stay in touch with that hiring manager.

1. Send a thank-you note

Most job hunters do send thank-you notes. You should send them too.

Keep in mind that businesses are formal. Manners are important. Thank-you notes are expected. Managers look for these things.

Keep your thank-you note brief.

- Thank the manager for meeting with you and mention the date and job title you interviewed for.
- Say that you want the job.
- Give one or two solid reasons why the hiring manager should offer you the job.
- Offer the manager a thirty-day trial period to prove yourself.
- Say that you'd like to call in a week or so to see if she's made a decision.

Write your thank-you note and send it off within 24 hours of the interview so the manager will remember who you are.

2. Send an idea note

Now, here's something hardly any of your competitors will try—

During your interview, the manager asked if you had any questions for her. You said, "Yes, what are the major challenges the new hire will face in this job?"

Now, think about the manager's answer. If the problems are not confidential, discuss them with a friend or look for a solution online. Come up with a few suggestions. Then, send

Fifty-five percent of job hunters send thank-you notes to the people who interviewed them.

—Vault.com

the manager a short note explaining your ideas.

Your suggestions don't have to be brilliant, just good. The point is, the manager will see that you're a problem solver and that you were the only one who made an extra effort to win the job offer.

Send your idea note a day or so after your thank-you note, but before you follow-up on the telephone.

3. Call the manager

A week after your interview, call the manager to see if she's made a decision. Yes, everybody hates making these calls. But, it shows that you're the kind of person who gets things done—even if the task is unpleasant. Use the calling script on the right.

4. If you didn't get the job, stay in touch

Once or twice a month, send every hiring manager you've interviewed a short note and another copy of your resume. Let them know that you are still available and that you are still interested in working for them.

Remember, jobs open up all the time. Some people decline job offers. Some change their minds and quit. Other people don't work out and management moves to replace them.

Sometimes jobs also open up in other departments as well. Most managers are eager to refer solid applicants to other hiring managers.

So, stay in touch with all your hiring managers. They are your inside connection—and a gentle persistence can re-open doors. The idea is to become the first person they think of when something new opens up.

—Best wishes, Harry Dahlstrom

CALL THE HIRING MANAGER AND SEE IF YOU GOT THE JOB

Call the manager and introduce yourself.

"Good morning, Ms. Hireyou. This is Emma Gogetter. I wanted to call and thank you for meeting with me last week about your lion tamer's position."

Ask if the manager has made a decision.

"I'm very interested in that position and I thought I might follow-up to see if you've made a decision."

If you got the job—

"Really? Yikes! Hey Ma..."

"When would you like me to start?"

"What time should I report?"

"Where should I report?"

"To whom should I report?"

"What do I need to bring with me on the first day?"

If the manager hasn't yet made a decision—

"Am I still a candidate for consideration?"

"I would love to have this job. Would you consider giving me a trial period to prove myself?"

If she needs time to think it over, ask—"Would it be okay if I call back on Friday?"

If you didn't get the job—

Don't beg, don't lose your cool, and don't close any doors. You might say—

"Gee, I'm sorry to hear that."

"Ms. Hireyou, I'd like to thank you for your time and consideration. It was a pleasure to meet you and to learn about your company."

"If the person you chose for this job becomes unavailable, please call me. I'd be happy to come in for another interview."

CPSIA information can be obtained
at www.ICGtesting.com
Printed in the USA
LVHW01s1451060418
572582LV00001B/53/P

9 780940 712997